GIRLS' LIFE MAGAZINE

GL The Girls' Life Guide to Great Parties

Edited by Kelly White

Illustrated by Lisa Parrett

Scholastic Inc.

New York • Toronto • London • Auckland • Sydney
Mexico City • New Delhi • Hong Kong • Buenos Aires

ISBN 0-439-44980-4

Design: Mark Neston

12 11 10 9 8 7 6   6 7 8/0

Printed in the U.S.A.

First Scholastic printing, June 2003

Contents

It's Party Time!

Nothing beats getting together with your pals, right? Whether it's just you and your BFF having a perfect slumber party or you're throwing a super-big birthday bash, parties are supposed to be, well, fun! From pre-party prep and fabulous food ideas to games galore, decorations, and more, *The Girls' Life Guide to Great Parties* shows you how to throw a party with pizzazz...or a fiesta with punch! Whatever the season (or even for no reason), be the girl who throws the party that everyone can't stop talking about. Can't wait to celebrate? Somebody get this party started!

Karen

Karen Bokram
Editor-in-Chief, *GL*

Chapter 1

Be a Girl with a Party Plan

Bet you'd love to throw the party of the year—the one that leaves your friends buzzing for weeks. You can! All it takes is a little organization, thinking ahead, and a smile. Sounds basic, but sometimes parties fall flat because girls get too caught up in throwing the "perfect" party and accidentally miss out on all the fun. But much of the excitement of throwing a party can be *before* the bash: figuring out how to decorate, what activities to plan, and which foods to fix and serve. So here's how to throw the most awesome fiesta of the year and how to have the best time while you're at it.

FIRST THINGS FIRST

Go see your 'rents. Face it—you can't throw a bash without their help. Parties take time to plan, and, of course, they cost money. Your folks are the ones who have to part with the dough, so whatever they say goes. Keep in mind that you *can* make some money-conscious contributions, too, such as creating your own invites and keeping the guest list to a minimum.

SPEAKING OF...

Coming up with a guest list can be a sensitive task, especially if your parents put a limit on how many friends you are allowed to invite. The last thing you want to do is hurt anybody's feelings.

There are a few ways to handle this sitch delicately. Say you're planning a backyard barbecue and you want to invite half the class, but your parents say, "No way!" If you had boys on your guest list, consider making it an all-girl party. Boys won't be bummed about not being invited to a party that's girls-only.

If your guest list is going over the limit by just one or two buds, talk to your parents about possibly stretching the rules a bit. And if they won't bend? Whittle the list down to your closest friends, and try to plan something fun for another day with the girls you had to cut.

Also, don't hand out invites in front of the kids who aren't invited—no one wants to know that she isn't being included in some upcoming fun. (And, it goes without saying that it's just plain mean to invite a whole bunch of buds to a bash and deliberately exclude certain others.)

WHEN?

Having a party on a school night definitely isn't recommended. But even when planning a weekend gathering, check the calendar to make sure nothing else major is happening at the same time—a school dance, a big athletic event, or, worst of all, someone else's party.

Also, even though meteorologists aren't always so great at predicting the weather, consider what the conditions might be like in your area on your potential party day—especially if you're opting for an outdoor bash. It wouldn't hurt to have a backup plan in the event of an unexpected downpour. (Rain date, anyone?) And again, it's entirely up to your folks to approve (or veto) whatever party date you choose.

WHERE?

Once you get the lowdown from your folks on what you can spend, what day is most convenient, and how many guests you can host, head to your favorite thinking spot with a pen and some paper—then brainstorm!

Your first question should be whether you want to have your party at home. If you do, there are theme parties, sleepover parties, or any other type of party that pleases you. (There are plenty of suggestions in the following chapters to give you some food for thought.) Just pick a room in which to host your event, and make sure there's enough space for everyone to sit and be comfortable.

If you decide to host your shebang out of the house, there are tons of options on where to go. Here are just a few:

✳ **On the Air:** Plan for you and your pals to go to a local radio station and take the grand tour. Guides will show you what goes on—chaos included—behind the scenes. You'll see how reporters gather and broadcast news. Did you know that some on-camera TV anchorwomen wear professional blouses and jackets with sweatpants and socks while broadcasting? Well, hey, you can't see under those desks from your TV screen! Visit a radio station and see how DJ's choose songs. Did you know music is usually picked out and ready to roll before the DJ hits his chair? Many DJ's can tell you exactly how long your fave songs take to play. They'll probably play a birthday request, if you ask nicely. Call local stations to find out the scoop.

✳ **Hit the Water:** If you've lucked into having a birthday during warm weather, take full advantage. Go to a nearby beach (at the shore or a lake, if you live near one), or look into renting a local swimming pool for the day (unless you happen to have one in your backyard). If you're renting a pool, be sure to hire a lifeguard. If you're at the beach, ask all your guests to bring pails and shovels (you're never too old) and have a sand sculpture contest. Sand castles are fine and good, but how about making a sand turkey? Or monster? Or pair of sneakers? Don't forget to bring your CD player and plenty of good tunes.

* **Back to the Future:** Some laser tag arenas can be rented out for birthday parties. So grab a zapper, don a shield, and head into a futuristic city to do virtual combat with your friends. How 21st century! The atmosphere is cosmically cool, and you and your buds will have a blast playing this high-tech version of the classic game of Tag. Your party will definitely go off with a bang.

Here Are Some More Ideas For Outta-House Party Places:

* zoo
* movie theater
* water park
* children's museum
* bowling alley
* arcade
* rec center

* amusement park
* campground
* theme restaurant
* go-cart track
* horseback riding farm
* miniature golf course

INVITING INVITES

Invitations should be mailed two to three weeks before the party. Be absolutely sure to include all the party nitty-gritty: Where, what day, what time, the occasion, and your name, of course, so guests know who's throwing the party. And ask your guests to RSVP by a specific date so you'll know how many people to expect. RSVP stands for *repondez s'il vous plait*. That's "respond if you please" in French.

To avoid having party-goers who don't know when to leave, include what time the party ends along with the time it starts. Some people don't know when to call it a night, and you don't want any stragglers wearing out their (or your folks') welcome.

You can go for store-bought invitations, but you'll save money and give your party a personal touch by making your own. And you don't have to be a skilled graphic designer to do so. If you've chosen a theme, your invitation should tie into it. For example, decorate your invitation to look like a piece of pizza, safari animal, baseball glove, tree—whatever goes with your theme.

Artistic types can draw an original design and photocopy it onto colored paper. Fill in the designs with paints, markers, and colored pencils. Sequins and glitter are fun, too, except they're messy and nearly impossible to clean from the carpet (so please put newspaper on your work surface!). But, they do scream "Party!" For an extra-festive (less messy) touch, throw a handful of confetti inside each envelope before sealing.

If you have a color printer, you can design invitations on your computer. You can also go to a greeting card Web site for e-invitations—pick one, fill in the blanks, and shoot them off to the kids on your guest list (assuming everyone you're inviting has an e-mail address). Or, print 'em off and pop 'em in the mail. Here are some other ideas for making unique invitations:

✳ **Candy Bar Wrapper:** Buy a bunch of candy bars that are plain white on the underside of the paper wrapper. Take the paper off the bar, leaving the foil in place. Write the party details inside the paper wrapper, tape it back around the foil, pop the candy bar in an envelope, and mail it off.

✳ **Tape a Song:** If you're musically inclined, record a little ditty about your party and include all the pertinent info in the lyrics. Make copies on a dual-cassette tape player or burn it onto blank CD's, put them in padded envelopes, and send.

✳ **Strike a Pose:** You're more artistic than musical? Make photocopies of pictures of all your guests from a yearbook or class photo. Cut out their pictures from the photocopies and tape them to a party scene you've drawn on the invite card.

PRETTY PRESSED FLOWER INVITATIONS

Here's one more can't-miss idea for creating an amazing handmade invitation!

Pressed Flowers

What You Need:

* fresh flowers and/or leaves
* a phone book
* scrap paper
* something to write with
* heavy books

What You Do:

1. Depending on the season, pick fresh flowers from the garden (get permission first or buy an inexpensive assortment from your local grocery store) or collect some pretty leaves from outside. Make sure the flowers are not damp but dry, though not so dry that they're wilted.

2. Open a phone book near the back and place a flower and/or leaf facedown on the page (make sure the petals don't overlap!). Write the date on a piece of scrap paper (you'll want to press everything for at least a week), and mark the page with it. Place more flowers and/or leaves on other pages, marking each page with dated scrap paper.

3. Put the phone book in a warm, dry place, and pile several heavy books on top of it (more phone books or encyclopedias, for example).

4. Wait a week before checking. When the flowers and/or leaves don't stick to the pages, they're dry and ready to be removed and used.

Flower Card

What You Need:

* construction paper
* scissors
* glue
* markers

What You Do:

1. Take an 8-1/2 x 11-inch piece of construction paper. Fold the short sides to meet. Then fold the paper in half the other way. (Your card will be 4-1/4 x 5-1/2 inches.) Then, cut out flowers, stems, and leaves from construction paper.

2. Arrange your cut-outs on the front of the card, and use small dots of glue to hold everything in place. Or you can also carefully glue your pressed flowers or leaves to the front of your card.

3. Write the party info inside the card using markers, and slip the card into a homemade envelope (instructions follow) with some pretty pressed flowers (instructions above).

Homemade Envelope

What You Need:

- ✳ 8-1/2 x 11-inch piece of paper
- ✳ scissors
- ✳ glue
- ✳ stickers

What You Do:

1. Place your flower card sideways in the center of an 8-1/2 x 11-inch piece of paper.

2. Fold the 8-1/2-inch edge up over the card, and fold the top edge down to overlap the bottom edge that you just folded up.

3. Fold the 11-inch sides in around the card but not too tight—you want to be able to easily slip the card in and out of the envelope.

4. Unfold the paper, and set the card aside. Cut out the rectangles formed by the folds on all four corners of the paper.

5. Refold the envelope (without the card), folding in the 11-inch side pieces first. Apply glue on the side pieces to secure when you fold the bottom piece up. Let the envelope dry. (Be sure to keep the glue only on the edges, or your envelope will be glued shut.)

6. Insert your invite into the envelope. Seal each with a pretty sticker.

Party Dilemma: One of You Is Not Invited

It's *the* event of the season—*everyone* will be there! But wait, there's an invite missing. Guess who won't be the belle of the ball....

If it's your BFF who was left out: Call the hostess and ask her if by chance your BFF's invite got lost. If she says your BFF wasn't invited, you have two choices. One option is to RSVP that you'll be there, and then go and have a good time. The other is to thank the hostess for including you, but politely decline the invite. You've got other plans. You're spending that evening with your BFF.

If it's you who's left out in the cold: Could the invitation be lost in the mail? Did the hostess confuse your locker number? If your BFF was invited and you weren't, try and understand if she still wants to make the scene. You have plenty of notice, so make plans with other friends or family for a super fun night out. Chances are your BFF will feel guilty about going without you, but show her you know it's not her fault you weren't invited and have your own fun!

THE NAME GAME

Many say the art of throwing a cool party is knowing how to prevent bad scenes before they happen. You know that when everyone sits down for cake, Julie is going to be angry that she couldn't sit next to Stacie, who wanted to sit next to Allie. How to avoid the mess? Name cards. Just fold a small piece of construction paper (cut to about the size of an index card) in half lengthwise. With the fold at the top, write a guest's name in the center of the card and put a fun sticker in the corner for decoration. Place the name cards near the table settings for each guest. *You* determine the seating arrangement—no arguments. And if you decorate the tags, everyone has a little token to take home.

DECORATE GREAT

The kind of party you're throwing definitely dictates the décor (and there are plenty of ideas throughout this book). But be sure to go for colorful streamers, and never underestimate the effectiveness of balloons— lots of 'em! Mylar balloons are expensive, but who says you have to go with helium? Just blow up bunches and bunches of regular party balloons until they cover the floor of your party area. (Get plenty of help so you don't hyperventilate.) Some balloons will inevitably burst! But that's what makes a party go POP!

RENT A DAY OF FUN

Why not look in the Yellow Pages under "Amusement" and "Entertainers", or go with a recommendation from a friend? If your budget allows it, you can hire magicians, fortune-tellers, and DJ's to spark up the day. Find out what crazy game equipment you can afford to rent. While some rentals can be pricey, something as simple as a trampoline can really make a party. If you have a friend or sister with a birthday close to yours, consider having a double party—it's half the cost, twice the fun.

CHEESE, PLEASE!

You must, must, must snap lots and lots of photos at a party. The best pictures are the ones that aren't posed—those spontaneous shots you take when guests don't realize they're being photographed. Polaroid cameras are great for parties because you can watch the *instant* photos develop before your very eyes. And digital cameras are great fun too, if you have a computer handy.

Polaroid shots also make great party favors. Ask one of your folks to be in charge of snapping pics of you with all your buds during the party. Then slip each photo into an inexpensive refrigerator magnet frame (those clear plastic ones with magnetic strips on the back) and write the date of the party and something personal ("Love, Megan") on it in colorful paint-pens. Give a magnet to each of your buds as a take-home gift.

Want lots of fun photos to remember the party? Then plan a party scrapbook or album. Hand out disposable cameras to the guests as they arrive—ask them to snap fun shots during your bash, then collect the cameras at the end. Get all the photos developed and you'll have a huge stack of shots—enough to fill a scrapbook. Share extras with friends.

MUSIC WORKS MAGIC

Music sets the party tone like nothing else. Be sure to have the stereo cranking before guests arrive—not too loud. You want your friends to be able to chat! Try to match the music to the party theme if you can. If you're having a hoedown, spin country tunes. You're hosting a '70s party? Play disco. Mixed CD's are great for parties—they really shake things up and cater to everyone's musical tastes. Once all the guests arrive, you could always start with a quick, informal game of Name That Tune to break the ice. And when things really get going, turn up the volume a notch or two and catch a good case of dance fever.

Hip Party Tip

If you're having your bash outside, remember that sound travels...right into your neighbors' houses. Just remember that next-door neighbors might not be as overjoyed as your guests to hear your party jams blaring at full blast. So be considerate and keep the volume reasonable. You want to be able to crank it up? You could always invite your neighbors to the party! Or have the party at a place like a rec center that can absorb loud music.

DO GUESTS A FAVOR

Party favors are the bags of fun stuff you give each guest to take home. One idea: Start with a whole bunch of colorful candies, or other small, colorful items (like pretty glittery beads for friendship bracelets). Open a piece of tissue paper on the counter, place a handful of your colorful collection in the middle, gather all four corners to the center, and tie with a fancy piece of ribbon to hold in place. Hand out the little goody sachets at the end of the party.

BOOK IT!

Get a small blank journal, and label it your guest book. As friends leave, have each of them dedicate a page in the book to your party. They can sign their names, write a sentence or two about what a blast they had, draw a picture, whatever. Don't forget to have a pen handy—or an assortment of pens, if you want your guest book to be a color-packed keepsake. Oh, and you should sign, too!

PARTY COUNTDOWN

You know how you always put that social studies project off to the last minute, then scramble around to pull it all together? Don't do that for your party. Get a head start. Pencil out a detailed overall to-do list, and make sure you include two shopping trips on that list—one for supplies and the other for food. (Don't forget paper products for quick and easy cleanup!) Here's a countdown to help you map everything out....

Three Weeks Ahead

✻ Put together your guest list.

✻ Plan your menu (more on that in Chapters 3 through 7).

✻ Figure out what games and activities you'll plan for your party (check out Chapters 2 through 7).

✻ Make a list of party supplies (streamers, balloons, favors) and any materials you'll need to make invites, decorations, crafts, and name cards.

Two Weeks Ahead

✻ Hit the craft and party supplies stores for the things on your list.

✻ Make one-of-a-kind invites and mail them.

One Week Ahead

* Make a grocery list.
* Make any party decorations that have to be crafted in advance.

Two to Three Days Ahead

* Go grocery shopping.
* Clean the house (if your party is being held at home).

Day Before the Party

* Prepare any food that can be made ahead of time.
* Decorate the party room (if your party is at home—if away, call the party place to confirm the date and time).

Party Day

* Store away any household items that could easily get broken.
* Take care of last-minute food prep. (Be sure to have plenty of ice on hand for cold drinks.)
* Have fun!

Picture Perfect

Those dreaded words: "I forgot to get film!" The party's in full swing, you're having the time of your life, and you want to remember it forever. So you break out the camera, but...it's not loaded. Word to the wise: Don't forget to get film ahead of time (or go digital)!

Chapter 2

No More Wallflower Hour

You're having your party at the skating rink? Things should be rolling right along. You're getting together for mini-golf? The party ought to take its course. But if you're having a bash at your house, at a hall, or even in a park, you and your buds can't just sit there and stare at each other. It's up to you to plan some fun stuff to do at your fiesta.

LET THE GAMES BEGIN

To really get things going, have games at your bash. You can break out classic party games like Pictionary or Twister, or go with some of the other suggestions throughout this book. Tweak standard party activities like Musical Chairs by having everyone walk backward around the chairs. Or instead of Pin the Tail on the Donkey, how about Pin the Mustache on the Math Teacher? Instead of Hide-and-Seek, try Seek-and-Hide....

SEEK-AND-HIDE

How to Play:

* One person hides in a secret spot.

* After counting to 10, everyone sets off in search of the hider. Whoever finds the hider joins that person in the hiding spot. When someone else finds the two of you, she joins in the hiding, too!

* The first one to find the hider is the winner. But, the game isn't over until everyone is crowded together in the hiding place.

ZANY BRAINY BALLOON RACE

How to Play:

* Ask guests to pair off in twos, and line partners up on one side of the party area.

* Partners face each other and sandwich a blown-up balloon between their foreheads.

* The first team to the other side of the room or yard—without popping or dropping the balloon—wins! But, no hands! If your balloon pops, you're disqualified. Harder yet, if the balloon gets away, you have to try to pick it up again—still no hands!

WET-N-WILD WATER TAG

How to Play:

* This one is great when played outdoors in hot weather. Assign one person to be It.

* Whoever's It fills a tall plastic cup with water, and should have access to an outside faucet for refills.

* Play the game just like traditional Tag, but instead of tagging the other players, the person who is It tosses water from the cup at the other players.

* Last player to stay dry is the winner. Or, once It drenches someone, that person becomes It, until everyone is soaking wet.

Pull the Plug!

Unless you're waiting for the ball to drop on New Year's Eve or you're watching a big tennis match, unplug the TV. Nothing dampens the spirits of a good party more than a group of guests glued to the tube.

EYE ON THE PRIZE

If you want to award the winners of the games, definitely hit the dollar store beforehand for great, cheap prizes. Here are some inexpensive prize suggestions:

* hair scrunchies
* candy bars
* notebooks
* lip glosses
* funky pencils

* friendship bracelets
* cool erasers
* mini puzzles
* bottles of nail polish

* fun socks
* sun visors
* bath fizzies
* superballs
* stickers

GET CRAFTY!

Doing crafts together is an excellent activity—and it guarantees your guests will have something really cool to take home. If you're going to do a craft at your party, make sure you have enough supplies to go around. Also, be sure to have ample work space and seating. And, please, put down plenty of newspaper to offset any messy mishaps. Definitely have a grownup on hand to supervise, too, especially when using sharp stuff such as scissors, sewing needles, and pliers. This book is packed throughout with unbeatable craft projects, and here are a few good ones to give any party a creative kick!

Stuffy T-Cushion

You know that T-shirt you've outgrown but just can't part with? Turn it into a pillow! Have everyone bring their fave too-tiny-to-wear tees to the party.

What You Need:

* thick-gauge thread
* sewing needle (with an eye big enough for the thread to fit through)
* old too-tiny T-shirt
* scissors
* pillow stuffing (from fabric store or craft store)
* an adult to help

What You Do:

1. Thread the needle and knot the thread. Use a basic over-and-under stitch to sew closed the neck and sleeves of your T-shirt.

2. Put stuffing inside the shirt until it's puffy, being sure to stuff the sleeves, too.

3. Use the same over-and-under stitch to close up the bottom of the shirt.

Festive Fabric Frame

This is a great party craft because guests can frame a picture from the party.

What You Need:

* sturdy cardboard
* newspaper
* X-ACTO knife
* ruler
* pencil
* glue
* bright, funky-patterned paper (like wrapping paper)
* scissors
* tape
* an adult to help

What You Do:

1. To make a frame for a 4 x 6-inch photo, place some cardboard on newspaper. Have an adult use an X-ACTO knife to cut out one 6 x 8-inch rectangle and one 5 x 7-inch rectangle from the cardboard. It's a good idea

Step 1
(for an adult
to do)

to have this part done before your guests arrive. Cut out enough for each guest.

2. Measure in 1-1/4 inches from all four sides of the 6 x 8-inch rectangle and draw lines all the way across to make a smaller inner rectangle. This will become the opening for your frame. Cut out the inner rectangle.

3. Layout flat an 8-1/2 x 11-inch piece of funky paper. Then, thinly spread glue onto the 6 x 8-inch frame—this will be the back side of your cardboard frame. Center it on the paper, glued side down. Smooth it out and let it dry.

Step 4

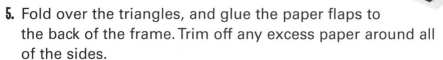

4. With scissors, poke a hole in the center of the paper, and cut diagonally to each corner of the frame's opening (you'll make an X shape).

5. Fold over the triangles, and glue the paper flaps to the back of the frame. Trim off any excess paper around all of the sides.

6. Lay the 6 x 8-inch frame down so that the back faces up. Lay the 5 x 7-inch rectangle over the 6 x 8-inch frame (covering the cut-out hole) and tape around three sides with tape (strong stuff like duct tape works well). Tape accordingly, depending on whether the frame sits upright or sideways. Or glue the two cardboard pieces together (but leave an opening to slide your picture in).

Step 6

7. Slide a photo into the back slot and, if necessary, tape it shut.

8. To make a stand, cut a 1-1/2 x 7-1/2-inch piece of cardboard. Measure down 2 inches from one end and make a bend there. Glue the bent part near the top of the frame so that the bottom of the stand is lined up with the bottom of the frame (make sure it stands evenly without rocking!).

Step 8

Note: *If you want, you and your friends can further fancy-up your frames with paints, glitter, sequins, buttons, silk flowers, sea shells, or whatever.*

Wonderful Wired Wreaths

Wreaths are super easy to make—for any season!

What You Need:

* thin wire coat hanger
* pliers
* floral tape
* silk flowers and greens
* floral wire (from craft store)
* tacky glue
* wooden beads, buttons, or other decorations
* ribbon
* an adult to help

What You Do:

1. Use pliers to shape a wire coat hanger into a circle. Bend the hook part of the hanger into a loop for hanging your wreath.

2. Wrap the entire hanger, including the loop, in floral tape by winding the tape around and around the hanger until it's covered.

3. Cover the taped hanger with a layer of greens (dried eucalyptus works great) by placing the greens along the hanger and using pieces of floral wire to secure them.

4. Attach silk flowers and greens to the hanger with floral wire until your wreath is fully decorated.

5. Use tacky glue to secure any flowers or greens that won't stay in place or to add other decorations such as wooden beads or buttons. Finish off your handiwork with a ribbon to decorate the top or bottom of your wreath.

What You Can Do To Make Your Wreath Fit The Season:

* **Winter Holiday Wreath:** Use lots of garland, pinecones, nuts, small ornaments, cinnamon sticks, wooden or plastic berries. Spray with a light touch of artificial snow-in-a-can.

* **Valentine's Heart Wreath:** Rather than bending the wire hanger into a circle, shape it into a heart. Go for lots of red and pink flowers, and finish up with a little spritz of your favorite perfume.

* **Spring Has Sprung Wreath:** Choose pastel colors, and go with the stuff that sprouts early—tulips, daffodils, irises. Dangle little artificial birds or bunnies from the center.

* **Patriotic Wreath:** Try red roses, white baby's breath, and blue button flowers. Glue on miniature paper American flags (the kind that come on toothpicks in the party supplies store). Hang long pieces of red, white, and blue ribbon like streamers from the bottom of the wreath.

* **Awesome Autumn Wreath:** Use leaves in crisp fall colors—orange, red, brown, yellow. If you press fresh ones, they'll keep their color (see Pressed Flower instructions on page 8).

Time to Unwind

If you ever want your folks to let you host another soirée, you'd better (ugh) promise to clean up—and you need to keep that promise and clean up well. Prior to party day, enlist a best friend to stick around and help you mop up the post-party mess. You'll owe her big for this one. In exchange, offer to help her straighten up her room, or treat her to a private ice cream fest a few days afterward.

Chapter 3

In the Mood for Food

What's cookin'? Guests tend to work up an appetite at parties. Even if you think your culinary skills are limited to peanut butter and jelly, you can whip up a great party spread to impress your friends!

MEET THE MUNCHIES

Before your guests arrive, set out some munchies—bowls of pretzels, chips and salsa, and trays of appetizers like baby carrots with veggie dip. It'll give the gals (and guys, if it's a girl/boy bash) something to munch on as you mingle and await everyone's arrival. Oh, and keep the snacks and appetizers light if you're serving a main course. Don't want everyone to fill up before the feast!

MENU MADNESS

Sit down and figure out what kind of food you want to serve—even if it's just cake and ice cream. If you're going for more of an all-you-can-eat buffet (or something in between), you can choose from a number of different courses—appetizers, entrees, side dishes, desserts. And let's not forget about thirst-quenching—beverages are a must at *any* party.

Oh, and one more word of advice: Buy ice! Your refrigerator's ice maker won't be able to keep up with the demand.

Choose your recipes wisely (like, don't pick two dishes that have to be baked at the same time but at different temperatures) and read them carefully. Make a list of all the ingredients you need from the grocery store, and make sure you have all the necessary cookware—proper-sized pots, pans, and utensils.

Figure out what you can (and should) make ahead of time (such as cake), what you can make ahead and reheat the day of the party (most casseroles), and what's best whipped up on the party day (punch).

And always pay attention to how much food a particular recipe makes. If it serves 10 people, but you're only having 5 guests, cut the measurements in half. Likewise, if a recipe serves 5 and you're having 10, double the quantities! When adjusting a recipe, you might also need to ask an adult for help, as well—to tweak cooking time and the size of the cookware you're using.

Don't Get Spoiled

For outdoor parties, chill leftover food in a cooler or bring it inside and refrigerate. It's not safe to leave food out in the heat—it goes bad fast. You can put out bowls of candy to fend off serious cases of the post-meal munchies.

PIZZA, THE PARTY STAPLE

No time to cook? Order takeout! Pizza has long been the perfect party food. It's just a phone call away, relatively inexpensive, easy to clean up, and no silverware required. What could be better? Even some of the frozen varieties are decent, and you can always doctor up the pizza with whatever toppings you want.

Better yet, make your own pizzas—quick, easy, and delicious. No, we don't expect you to toss dough. Get pre-made pizza crusts, or use large tortillas (great for Mexican pizza), extra-big pita breads (get 'em in gourmet stores), or focaccia (try your bakery). Smear your crust with tomato marinara, pizza sauce, salsa, or canned crushed tomatoes.

Season the pizza with oregano, Italian seasoning, basil, onion, garlic, or crushed red pepper. Sprinkle with shredded cheese—any kind you like— and load up on your favorite toppings. Pepperoni, anyone? Or try a few pizza combos you've never had before. These are some of our faves:

* mozzarella, feta, spinach, and mushrooms
* mozzarella, Parmesan, and fresh tomato
* Monterey Jack, cheddar, black beans, and black olives
* provolone, mozzarella, and ricotta cheese

Note: *Cook pizzas at 450° for about 10 minutes.*

BRING IT ON

It's perfectly OK to ask a couple of your close pals to bring a dish to your party. Your bud Anna makes the best-ever cheese dip? Great! Ask if she wouldn't mind bringing it along. You can even take it a step further and throw a Potluck Party and ask *everyone* to bring a dish. Be sure to remember to assign each person a different course or dish (you don't want to end up with four salads and no dessert!).

And be sure to let your pals know how many guests you're expecting. Your party is an all-out bash? No one should have to make something that's more than six or eight servings, so double up (have two girls each bring a lasagna, or have two girls each bring brownies) or even ask for variations on the same item (one girl brings garlic bread, another one cheesy Parmesan bread—you get the idea!).

EASY BAKE

You can always opt to buy ready-made stuff or get takeout. For instance, in the grocery freezer section you can find lasagnas that will feed a crowd. All ya do is reheat. Feel like an Asian theme? Order up some fried rice and fortune cookies for a pre-made party.

The most popular party staple is cake. If your local bakery makes the most awesome double chocolate layer cake, go for it—if it's affordable. Keep in mind that you might have to order the cake a few days in advance, especially if you need enough to feed a small army.

Still want to make the food at home? There are ways to cut down on kitchen time, too. If a recipe calls for shredded carrots, for instance, you can pick up pre-shredded packs from the produce department.

Forget something? If a recipe calls for an ingredient you don't have on hand, substitute it with something fittingly similar (cheddar cheese instead of Monterey Jack, or wheat bread for sandwiches instead of white, for example). Keep that in mind when making any of the yummy all-purpose party recipes that follow....

APPETIZERS

Some people call 'em *hors d'oeuvers* (pronounced "or-derves"), meaning "outside of the main course." Whatever you call them, they're the foods you put out before the rest of the meal is served to fend off hunger pangs and growling stomachs.

Inside-Out Mini-Pizzas

makes 20

They're kind of like little calzones!

What You Need:

* 1 cup shredded mozzarella
* 1/2 cup chopped pepperoni
* 1/2 cup tomato sauce
* 1 tablespoon oregano
* 1 teaspoon garlic powder
* 20 refrigerator biscuits
* 1 egg, beaten
* 1/4 cup grated Parmesan

* measuring cups and spoons
* flour for dusting your work surface
* bowl
* a drinking glass
* spoon
* baking sheet

What You Do:

1. Preheat the oven to 350°.

2. Mix mozzarella, chopped pepperoni, tomato sauce, oregano, and garlic powder in a bowl.

3. Separate the biscuits. On a lightly floured work surface, use the bottom of a drinking glass (dip it in flour too) to flatten the biscuits into circles about 4 inches in diameter.

4. Spoon a heaping tablespoon of the sauce in the center of each circle. Pull up the biscuit so the sauce is sandwiched inside, and pinch the edges together.

5. Brush the tops of the biscuits with the beaten egg. Put them on a baking sheet and bake for 10 to 12 minutes, until golden.

6. Sprinkle grated Parmesan cheese on top to taste.

Happy Trail Mix

makes 4-1/2 cups

This is way more original (and more healthful) than that cereal box party mix stuff.

What You Need:

* 2 cups raisins
* 3/4 cup chocolate chips
* 1 cup shelled nuts like peanuts, walnuts, pecans, cashews, or a mixture
* 1/2 cup shredded coconut
* 1/4 cup sunflower seeds
* measuring cups
* bowl
* airtight container

What You Do:

1. Mix all ingredients in a bowl.

2. Put in an airtight container to store.

Bacon Breadstick Twists

makes 24

For a pretty presentation, make a bacon breadstick "bouquet" by serving these twists upright in a clean, shallow vase.

What You Need:

* raw bacon slices
* 24 breadsticks
* knife
* baking sheet
* shallow vase (for serving)

What You Do:

1. Preheat the oven to 375°.

2. Slice each piece of raw bacon lengthwise into two thin strips.

3. Twist strips around breadsticks from one end to the other (you'll use one strip per breadstick). Place them on a baking sheet.

4. Bake for 25 minutes or until the bacon is crisp.

Cheese Nibbles

If you're not throwing the party, but going to one, this is a great gift to bring the hostess. Wrap up the dough log in pretty plastic wrap, twist the wrapped ends, and tie some ribbon around them. All the hostess has to do is slice, bake, and serve.

What You Need:

* 1 stick butter, softened
* 1/4 teaspoon salt
* 1 cup flour
* 2 cups shredded cheddar
* 3 tablespoons milk
* bowl
* measuring cups and spoons
* plastic wrap
* knife
* baking sheet

What You Do:

1. Combine all ingredients (add milk last) in a bowl. Mix well.
2. Roll the mixture into two 12-inch long dough logs.
3. Wrap the dough in plastic wrap, and refrigerate overnight.

To Serve:

Preheat the oven to 375°. Slice cheese dough into rounds 1/4-inch thick, arrange on a baking sheet, and bake for 5 to 8 minutes.

ENTRÉES

The entrée is the biggest part of your meal—the main event. When planning your menu, it's a good idea to decide first on an entrée. Then, choose other dishes that make good accompaniments.

Lasagna Twirls

This is a perfect main course for an Italian-style meal (see Menu Mania! on page 32).

What You Need:

* 16 uncooked lasagna noodles
* 2 cups shredded mozzarella
* 2-1/2 cups ricotta
* 1 egg, beaten
* 2 tablespoons oregano
* 2 26-ounce jars pasta sauce
* 1 cup grated Parmesan

* saucepan
* bowl
* spoon
* measuring cups and spoons
* baking pan
* plastic wrap
* aluminum foil

What You Do:

1. Cook noodles in a saucepan according to package directions. Be careful not to overcook—they'll split apart.

2. Combine shredded mozzarella, ricotta, egg, and oregano in a bowl.

3. Lay cooked noodles out flat and use a spoon to spread the mixture onto them. Starting from one end, roll up each noodle so that it looks like a spiral with wavy edges.

4. Place lasagna twirls in a baking pan, and pour both jars of pasta sauce on top of them.

5. Cover with plastic wrap and refrigerate.

To Serve:

Preheat the oven to 375°. Remove the plastic wrap and cover the pan with aluminum foil and bake for 45 minutes. Remove from the oven, sprinkle grated Parmesan on top, and bake again, uncovered, for 15 minutes more.

Soft Taco Roll-ups

makes 16

Throwing a Mexican fiesta (see Menu Mania! on page 32)? *¡Olé!*

What You Need:

* 1 can refried beans
* 8 10-inch tortillas
* 2 cups shredded Monterey Jack
* 1 cup salsa
* measuring cups

* saucepan
* spoon
* toothpicks
* knife

What You Do:

1. Warm refried beans in a saucepan according to can directions. Spread them on the tortillas using a spoon.

2. Drizzle with cheese and salsa, and roll up. Keep the taco roll-ups secure with a toothpick near each end. Cut each roll-up in half, and serve. (If you want, you can turn this into an appetizer by cutting the roll-ups into 1-inch pinwheel slices.

Easy Cheesy Macaroni

serves 4

Serve this up with some other American favorites (see Menu Mania! on page 32).

What You Need:

* 1 pound elbow macaroni
* 1/2 cup flour
* 4 cups milk
* 4 cups shredded cheddar
* 1/2 cup already grated Parmesan

* measuring cups and spoons
* saucepan
* 3-quart casserole dish
* whisk
* bowl
* wooden spoon

What You Do:

1. Preheat the oven to 375°.

2. Cook macaroni in a saucepan according to package directions. Drain and pour into a 3-quart casserole dish.

3. Whisk flour and 1 cup milk in a bowl until blended. Pour into the saucepan you just emptied.

4. Add the remaining 3 cups milk, and cook on the stove top over medium heat, stirring constantly with a wooden spoon, until the sauce comes to a boil and thickens.

5. Lower heat, and add shredded cheddar cheese, until melted.

6. Pour cheese sauce over the macaroni in the casserole dish, and mix.

7. Sprinkle grated Parmesan on top and bake for 35 minutes, until bubbly and browned.

MENU MANIA!

If you want to give your party an international flair, plan a menu around the dishes from a particular country. Here are some examples:

Italian Fare

Taste of Italy Popcorn (recipe on page 45)

Lasagna Twirls (recipe on page 30)

Fried Zucchini Crisps (recipe on page 33)

Garlic Bread (recipe on page 98)

Cannolis (purchased from a bakery)

Fruity Soda Pop (recipe on page 39)

Mexican Fiesta

Nachos served with bottled salsa (purchased from a grocery store)

Soft Taco Roll-ups (recipe on page 31)

Cornbread (from a mix)

Good 'Ol USA Fest

Potato Chips and Onion Dip (from a grocery store)

Fried Chicken (from the supermarket deli or your favorite fried chicken chain)

Easy Cheesy Macaroni (recipe on page 31)

All-American Broccoli Bake (recipe on page 34)

Refrigerator Buttermilk Biscuits (in the refrigerator section of the grocery store)

Baby Peanut Butter Balls (recipe on page 38)

Ice Cream Punch (recipe on page 39)

SIDE DISHES

Don't underestimate the importance of side dishes to round out your meal. Think of it as you would when you are trying to find the perfect accessory for an outfit. Your main course is the outfit, and your side dish is the accessory.

Fried Zucchini Crisps

serves 12

This also makes a nice appetizer.

What You Need:

* 1-1/2 cups grated Parmesan
* 4 eggs
* 4 tablespoons flour
* 1 teaspoon salt
* 1 teaspoon garlic powder
* 1/2 cup milk
* 4 large zucchini
* canola oil
* bottled ranch dressing
* bowl
* whisk
* knife (for slicing)
* paper towels
* deep pot
* fork (for dipping rounds in batter)
* metal slotted spoon
* measuring cups and spoons
* an adult to help

What You Do:

1. Combine Parmesan, eggs, flour, salt, garlic powder, and milk. Whisk until smooth. Cover the bowl, and refrigerate for 30 minutes.

2. Slice zucchini into 1/4-inch rounds. Pat slices dry with paper towels.

3. Have an adult heat canola oil in a deep pot on the stove top over medium heat. Your adult can test to see whether the oil is hot enough by putting drops of the Parmesan batter in it. When the batter sizzles up quickly, the oil is ready.

4. Using a fork, dip zucchini rounds in the batter and coat completely. Have your adult drop the rounds into oil.

5. When golden, remove the battered zucchini with a metal slotted spoon. (Be careful of splattering oil.) Drain on paper towels.

6. Serve with ranch dressing for dipping.

All-American Broccoli Bake

serves 12

Hate to eat your greens? Not when they're prepared American-style!

What You Need:

* 2 1-pound packages frozen broccoli florets
* 2 cans condensed cream of mushroom soup
* 4 tablespoons milk
* 1/2 pound American cheese, cut in small pieces
* 2 tablespoons mayonnaise
* 1/2 pound crushed cheese-flavored crackers
* saucepan
* 3-quart casserole dish
* measuring cups and spoons
* mixing spoon

What You Do:

1. Preheat the oven to 350°.

2. Cook the broccoli in a saucepan according to package directions.

3. Put the cooked broccoli in a 3-quart casserole dish. Stir 2 cans of soup, the milk, cheese, and mayonnaise into the broccoli.

4. Top with crushed crackers and bake, uncovered, for 30 minutes.

Rabbit Food

serves 12

What's up, doc? These tasty carrots make a yummy addition to any meal.

What You Need:

* 2-1/2 pounds baby carrots
* 3 tablespoons maple syrup
* 3 tablespoons butter
* large pot
* wooden spoon
* measuring spoons

What You Do:

1. Place the carrots in a large pot, and fill with water until the carrots are covered.

2. Boil until tender. Drain.

3. Add the maple syrup and butter. Stir until coated.

Party Potatoes

If you're serving a light entrée, such as salad or soup, this is a great dish to serve alongside because it fills up the hungry folks.

What You Need:

* ✳ 4 cups frozen hash brown potatoes, thawed
* ✳ 1/2 pound frozen sausages, browned and crumbled
* ✳ 1/2 cup milk
* ✳ 1/2 teaspoon salt
* ✳ 1/4 teaspoon pepper

* ✳ 1/4 teaspoon garlic powder
* ✳ 1 tablespoon butter, melted
* ✳ 1/2 teaspoon paprika
* ✳ measuring cups and spoons
* ✳ large bowl
* ✳ 9-inch pie plate
* ✳ plastic wrap

What You Do:

1. In a large bowl, combine the potatoes, crumbled sausage, milk, salt, pepper, and garlic powder. Transfer the ingredients to a greased 9-inch pie plate.

2. Drizzle the ingredients with melted butter, and sprinkle with paprika.

3. Cover the pie plate with plastic wrap, and refrigerate until the next day.

To Serve:

Bake at 350° for 35 to 45 minutes, uncovered, or until lightly browned.

DESSERTS

OK, the entrée is supposed to be the main event, but some might disagree. What's a party without dessert?

Hamburger Cake

serves 16

This is the perfect cake to have at a cookout!

What You Need:

* 1 yellow cake mix (plus ingredients it requires)
* 1 brownie mix (plus ingredients it requires)
* 1 can whipped chocolate frosting
* 2 tablespoons crispy rice cereal
* red and yellow decorator icing
* measuring cups and spoons
* wooden spoon
* 2 mixing bowls
* 2 8-inch round cake pans
* round-bottomed casserole dish
* wire cooling rack

What You Do:

1. Make the yellow cake batter in a mixing bowl according to the directions.

2. Grease and flour the cake pan *and* the casserole dish. Pour half the batter into one of the greased cake pans; pour the other half into the casserole dish with a rounded bottom.

3. Mix the brownie batter in the other mixing bowl and pour into the second greased 8-inch round cake pan. Bake according to the directions on the box. When done, transfer to a wire rack to cool completely.

4. Bake the cakes. Once cool, frost the yellow cake that was baked in the pan. This will be the bottom of your "hamburger bun."

5. Place the brownie as your burger on top of the frosted cake.

6. Put the cake from the casserole dish on top of the brownie, rounded side up. Frost it.

7. Sprinkle the top of the cake with rice cereal for "sesame seeds."

8. Decorate the edges with the decorator icing for "ketchup" and "mustard," being sure to make some drip down the sides.

Rocky Road Clusters

Mmmm...not much more to say about this delicious confection.

What You Need:

* 1 12-ounce package semisweet chocolate chips
* 1 14-ounce can sweetened condensed milk
* 1 16-ounce package miniature marshmallows
* 2 cups dry roasted peanuts

* 9 x 13-inch baking dish
* medium saucepan
* wooden spoon
* large bowl
* plastic wrap
* measuring cups

What You Do:

1. Lightly grease a 9 x 13-inch baking dish.

2. In a medium saucepan over low heat, combine the chocolate chips and the milk. Stir until the chips are melted and the mixture is smooth. Meanwhile, combine the marshmallows and the peanuts in a large bowl.

3. When the chocolate mixture is melted, add it to the large bowl, over the marshmallows and nuts, and mix.

4. Pour the cluster mixture into the greased baking dish, cover with plastic wrap, and refrigerate for 2 hours.

5. Break into bite-sized pieces before serving.

Arctic Chocolate Pie

serves 8

It's awesome on a hot day—just be sure to serve right away, or you could wind up with Arctic Chocolate Soup!

What You Need:

* 1 quart chocolate ice cream
* 1 chocolate ready-made pie shell

* 1/4 cup chocolate syrup
* chocolate chips
* ice cream scoop
* measuring cups

What You Do:

1. Let the chocolate ice cream sit out for 5 minutes, so it's soft enough to serve.

2. Scoop the ice cream into the pie shell. Keep pressing the ice cream down with the back of the ice cream scoop until the shell is full and the ice cream forms a slight hump in the middle.

3. Drizzle chocolate syrup on top of the pie in a zig-zag design. Decorate a border of the pie with chocolate chips.

4. Freeze at least 1 hour.

Baby Peanut Butter Balls

makes 30

You don't even need to be having a party to make and enjoy these.

What You Need:

* 1/2 cup peanut butter
* 3 tablespoons butter, softened
* 1 cup sifted powdered sugar
* mini chocolate chips
* shredded coconut
* cocoa powder
* powdered sugar for coating
* measuring cups and spoons
* spoon
* bowl

What You Do:

1. Using a spoon, mix the peanut butter and the butter in a bowl.

2. Gradually stir in the cup of sifted powdered sugar, mini chocolate chips, shredded coconut, and cocoa powder, until well combined.

3. Roll the mixture into 1-inch balls. Then, the balls in toppings to coat— like some powdered sugar or cocoa powder (use as much as you'd like).

BEVERAGES

Your guests are going to need something to wash down all that food. Thirsty, anyone?

Fruity Soda Pop

serves 6

You can stock up on sodas, or you can make your own!

What You Need:

* 12-ounce can frozen juice concentrate, any flavor
* 2 1-liter bottles seltzer water
* ice
* large pitcher

What You Do:

1. Pour juice concentrate into a large pitcher.
2. Fill the empty juice can with seltzer water, and add to the pitcher six times.
3. Serve over ice. This won't stay bubbly long, so make it the day of the party.

Ice Cream Punch

serves 16

Ice cream in a drink? What could be better?

What You Need:

* 1 quart vanilla ice cream or any flavor sherbet
* 3/4 cup cold water
* 12-ounce can frozen lemonade concentrate, thawed
* 1-liter bottle lemon-lime soda
* measuring cups
* ice cream scoop
* punch bowl
* large spoon

What You Do:

1. Scoop the ice cream or the sherbet into the punch bowl.
2. Add water and lemonade concentrate, and stir gently with a large spoon.
3. Slowly pour in the lemon-lime soda, and again stir gently.

Fresh Lemonade

serves 10

This is just as good as the stuff you get in the mall—but way cheaper!

What You Need:

- ✳ 10 lemons, cut in halves
- ✳ 8 cups water
- ✳ 1-1/2 cups sugar
- ✳ ice

- ✳ pitcher
- ✳ spoon
- ✳ measuring cups

What You Do:

1. Squeeze the lemon halves over a pitcher to collect their juice (be sure to scoop out any seeds).

2. Add water and sugar.

3. With a spoon, stir until the sugar is dissolved. Serve over ice.

Note: *You can also try orangeade as an alternative. Just substitute oranges for lemons in the recipe above.*

Mind Your (Party) Table Manners

The only thing better than being a great host? Being a polite guest! It's important to be aware of table manners when you're at a party. Place your napkin on your lap, and use it to keep your mouth wiped. Eat only when every guest and the hostess have been served. If you don't like the food being offered, politely say, "No, thank you." If you want more to eat, ask the person closest to the dish to pass it to you—no leaning across the table. There isn't much point in mastering the etiquette of an embassy dinner, but you really should drop that elbows-on-the-table attitude. Speaking of elbows on the table...

The reason people don't put their elbows on the table is because in the old days it protected people from accidentally dunking their long, flowing sleeves into the gravy. Today, people follow the etiquette rule because nobody ever wants to stray from it and risk being considered rude.

Here's another traditional rule: Food is served from the left, and plates are cleared from the right. Do you know why? The rule was created eons ago so the servant in charge of serving didn't crash into the one in charge of clearing. This rule might appear to be silly today since servants are uncommon (although you are still served when dining out). OK, so maybe it's time we make some compromises—and update table manners. For instance, after the dishes are removed and the table swept free of crumbs, go ahead and put your elbows on the table. Why not?

Chapter 4

Super Slumber Parties

Nothing is better than a slumber party with your best gal pals! It's a party that doesn't end until the last girl drops off to sleep. Sleep? Yeah, right!

YOU'RE INVITED!

Make a sleepover invite with a keepsake Pipe Cleaner Party Doll. To make the sleeping bag, use an 8-1/2 x 11-inch piece of construction paper and fold it the long way. Then, cut 3 inches off (it should measure 5-1/2 x 8 inches). Fold it up three inches lengthwise, turn it over and write the party info on the back (the side without the flap). Use colored markers to draw designs—flowers, stars, whatever you like—on the sleeping bag front. Glue around the edges to close up the bag, being sure to leave an opening at the top of the flap. Above the fold, glue a square of pretty fabric as a pillow. Slip a tiny handmade Pipe Cleaner Party Doll inside before mailing off your invite in an envelope. Here's how to make the doll....

Pipe Cleaner Party Doll

What You Need:

* pipe cleaners
* ruler
* scissors
* embroidery floss in various colors (will be the doll's hair color and clothes, if you opt to make some)
* small wooden bead (with a big enough opening for your pipe cleaner to be doubled through)
* fine-point permanent marker

What You Do:

1. Cut one pipe cleaner to measure 6 inches and another pipe cleaner to measure 2 inches. Set them aside.

2. Cut three 6-inch strands of embroidery floss for the doll's hair.

3. Bend the 6-inch piece of pipe cleaner in half. Tie the floss at the bend.

4. Thread both ends of the pipe cleaner through the bead. Push the bead up to the bend, being sure to cover the place where you knotted the hair.

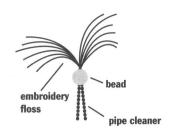

bead

embroidery floss

pipe cleaner

5. Twist the 2-inch piece of pipe cleaner once around the longer piece up near the bead to make the doll's arms.

6. Take the permanent marker, and draw a face on the bead. If you want, you can braid your doll's hair, tying the end with a colored floss bow. You can also wrap the doll in colored string to give her clothes.

PARTY CENTRAL

Dim the lights, have plenty of mixed CD's on hand, and pile up a bunch of pillows in the center of the room (be sure to choose a roomy room). Then make a "tent" out of streamers. Securely tape an even number of colorful streamers to the center of the ceiling. Take two streamers (they should be different colors) and twist them so the colors spiral. Then, pull the twisted streamer pairs (not too hard or they'll tear) to reach the far ends of the room. Tack the streamer ends to the floor by laying heavy books on top of them. Go around the room stretching the streamers until your "tent" is pitched. Just don't be upset when it falls apart after the party gets rollin'!

15 FUN THINGS TO DO ALL PARTY LONG WITH YOUR FRIENDS

You girls can curl up with some popcorn and videos later. But first, it's time to get silly with a bunch of wacky slumber party ideas. Sure, some take planning. And some you've heard of before. Heck, some are classics. And, yes, some are really over the top. But hey, that's the point.

1. See who can hula-hoop the longest.

2. Start with a huge bargain pack of bubble gum, and see who can blow the biggest bubble. When that gets old, see who can blow the biggest bubble to the slow count of four.

3. Have everyone come in the geekiest pajamas they can find. Whoever looks like the biggest dork is the winner!

4. Have a "*horror* d'oeuvre" contest. Get out the toothpicks and spear wacky food combos. Grossest nibble wins. Surprisingly, a pineapple chunk, cheddar cheese, Spam, and marshmallow combo isn't all that bad!

5. *Silly Party Game #1: Pass the Lifesaver.* Break the group into two teams and have each team form a line. Every player holds a toothpick in her mouth between her teeth. The first person on each team starts with a Lifesaver already on the toothpick. When someone says "Go!" the first person passes the Lifesaver to the second person without using her hands, and so on down the line. The Lifesaver goes down the line and back. The first team to finish wins.

6. *Silly Party Game #2: Shave the Balloon.* Each girl blows up a balloon, knots it closed, and smears it with shaving cream. Then, using a disposable plastic razor, she tries to shave the balloon clean without popping it. The girl left with an intact, clean-shaven balloon wins. If more than one girl still has an intact balloon once the shaving is finished, the girl who shaved the fastest wins!

7. Paint your fingernails and toenails in tacky fluorescents—a different color for each digit.

8. Find a book of old ghost stories, turn off all the lights, and shine a flashlight under your chin while you read them aloud.

9. Have a séance with a Ouija (pronounced "wee-jee") board. It's a slumber party classic. The board, available in any toy store, is marked with numbers, letters, and symbols—and comes with a movable pointer. Ask the "spirits" a question, and they supposedly respond by guiding your hands (while holding the pointer) to spell out the answer.

10. Get out board games you haven't played with since forever, or games your friends have never heard of that belonged to your older brothers or sisters. It's amazing how much fun a late-night game of Operation can be.

11. *Silly Party Game #3: Water Relay.* Break the group into two teams, forming two lines. The first person in each line holds a spoon. Place a bucket of water between the two lines. On the other side of the room, place a paper cup on a chair for each team. When someone says "Go!" the first person in each line must fill the spoon with water and rush over to pour it into their team's paper cup. The trick is to balance the spoon so the water doesn't spill. Then rush back and hand the spoon to the next player, who does the same thing. The team that fills their paper cup first wins. The game is best played in the basement.

12. Give each other silly makeovers with your mom's makeup (if she'll let you).

13. Have a pillow fight.

14. *Silly Party Game #4: Robe Reversal.* Pair everybody up with a partner. One partner wears a robe; the other one doesn't. Have partners face each other and hold hands. The girl wearing the robe has to get the robe off and onto her partner—while still holding hands. The first team to switch robes wins. (The robe will be inside-out and on backward once it's switched over.)

15. Have a silly hairdo contest. Get out the brushes, barrettes, hair ties, and—of course—hairspray!

MIDNIGHT SNACKS

Put bowls of snacks out for your late-night noshers—chips, trail mix, and plenty of fresh-popped popcorn. Popcorn loaded with melted butter and salt is delish, but try some of these other toppings, too....

✳ **Pepper Parm:** Sprinkle 1/4 cup of grated Parmesan cheese over hot popcorn, toss, and top with a few twists of a cracked-pepper mill.

✳ **Silly Chili:** Add a tablespoon of mild chili powder and a teaspoon of onion salt to hot popcorn. If your friends like it spicy, add a *pinch* of cayenne pepper before tossing.

✳ **Taste of Italy:** Mix a tablespoon of oregano or Italian seasoning with a teaspoon of garlic powder, and dust over hot popcorn. Toss.

✳ **Sweet Treat:** Mix 1/2 cup of pecans and 1/4 cup brown sugar with hot popcorn, and then sprinkle with 3 tablespoons of cinnamon.

✳ **Lemon-Herb:** Squeeze the juice from half a lemon into hot melted butter before drizzling over popcorn. Sprinkle with a dash of black pepper and a tablespoon of thyme.

PARTY SMARTY

Looking to give your slumber party a purpose? Here are some cool party ideas....

Craft Crash Bash: Have a craft party sleepover, either focusing on one craft or a whole bunch of different ones. You can make jewelry, photo frames, or bracelets. Or, you can try some other crafts recommended on the following pages. You can also opt to make your party a scrapbooking bash—everybody brings their photo albums and pics and stuff, and works together to share ideas. Or, you can have a collage get-together. Have everyone bring photos or old magazines to make collages on a variety of themes, such as fashion or sports.

TV Fest: No, you're not going to all sit around and zone out in front of the tube. Break out the videocam, and film your own reality show. Or record old movies, turn off the sound, and take turns "dubbing" the dialogue. You could also do improvisational skits—for example, give the group a box filled with interesting objects. Tell them they were all found in Aunt Erma's attic. Each girl or pair of girls gets five minutes to put together a story revealing why the seemingly unrelated objects explain a deep, dark family mystery. Tape the skits and watch them again to double the laughs. Or film two-minute scenes in separate rooms without knowing what anyone else has done. Then watch them pieced together as one weird story.

Never-Leave Vacation: Act like you're on vacation in your hometown. Take your group of girls out during the day to check out all the touristy things around your town that you rarely ever see—the art museum, science center, aquarium, whatever. At the end of the day, finish up like you're checking into a fine hotel—in your home—complete with mini toiletries, fancy towels and robes, and chocolate mints on each pillow.

CRAFT CRAZE

Here are a few craft ideas that are just perfecto for pulling off at a sleepover. String a clothesline across the party room to hang your creations with clothespins until dry.

Silly Sleep Shirts

What You Need:

* fabric paints, including the glitter kind
* extra-large plain white T-shirts (at least one per person)
* fabric glue
* sequins
* scissors
* fabric scraps

What You Do:

1. Use different fabric paints to color silly designs all over the T-shirts. Hang them to dry.

2. Accent the shirts by using fabric glue to secure sequins onto them (around the collar or sleeves or anywhere!).

3. Cut out designs, such as flowers or stars, from different fabric scraps, and glue them to the shirts.

Autographed Pillowcases

What You Need:

* plain white or light-colored pillowcases (one for each guest)
* permanent markers, in different colors

What You Do:

1. Each girl signs her name on her pillowcase using permanent markers in different colors.

2. Circulate the pillowcases to each other, and have each person draw some artwork and write an inspiring message to each other, such as, "You're one of the best buds ever."

3. Hang to dry.

Slipper Socks

What You Need:

* cotton socks in all different colors
* puffy fabric paint (available in craft stores)

What You Do:

1. Before the party, pre-wash the cotton socks and run them through the dryer.
2. Slip your hands into the socks so that the soles are pressed against your palms.
3. Decorate the soles with fabric paint.
4. Hang to dry. They should be ready to slip on your footsies by morning.

CHOW DOWN

A sleepover is not complete without some tasty treats in the AM.

Chocolate Waffles

serves 4

What You Need:

* 1-1/2 cups flour
* 1/3 cup unsweetened cocoa powder, sifted
* 1/3 cup sugar
* 1 tablespoon baking powder
* 1/4 teaspoon salt
* 2 egg yolks
* 1 teaspoon vanilla extract
* 1-3/4 cups milk
* 1/2 cup cooking oil

* 2 egg whites, beaten
* butter, berries, and powdered sugar (optional toppings)
* waffle iron
* 2 medium bowls
* whisk
* spoon
* small bowl
* fork
* an adult to help

What You Do:

1. Preheat your waffle iron.
2. In a medium bowl, combine the flour, sifted cocoa powder, sugar, baking powder, and salt.

3. In another medium bowl, beat the egg yolks (ask your adult to help you separate the egg yolks from the egg whites) and vanilla extract slightly using a whisk. Beat in the milk and oil. Then, add the egg mixture to the flour mixture. Stir until it's combined, yet still slightly lumpy.

4. With help from an adult, in a small bowl, beat the egg whites with a whisk until a stiff peak forms. Gently fold the beaten egg whites into the batter, leaving little fluffs of egg white. Be careful not to over-mix.

5. Pour some batter onto the grids of the slightly greased waffle iron. Close lid quickly. When the waffles are done, remove them with a fork. If you like, top the waffles with butter, berries, and powdered sugar.

Raisin-Bran Muffins

makes 24—make batter ahead

If you feel like having something lighter than waffles, bake muffins the morning of the sleepover and eat 'em along with your fave style of eggs.

What You Need:

* 3 cups whole bran cereal
* 1 cup boiling water
* 2 eggs, lightly beaten
* 2 cups buttermilk
* 1/2 cup canola oil
* 1 cup raisins
* 2-1/2 teaspoons baking soda
* 1/2 teaspoon salt
* 1 cup sugar
* 2-1/2 cups flour
* spoon
* measuring cups and spoons
* 2 bowls
* plastic wrap
* 2 muffin pans (each with 12 cups)

What You Do:

1. In a bowl, mix the bran cereal with boiling water, stirring to moisten. Set aside until cool.

2. Add the eggs, buttermilk, oil, and raisins to the cereal. Mix well.

3. In another bowl, stir together the baking soda, salt, sugar, and flour until thoroughly blended. Stir into the cereal mixture.

4. Cover tightly with plastic wrap and refrigerate.

To Serve:

Preheat the oven to 425°. Spoon the batter into greased muffin pans, filling the cups 2/3 full. Bake for 18 to 20 minutes or until the muffin tops spring back when lightly touched. Serve warm.

BEDROOM BEACH BASH

Make a splash by throwing a beach party in your bedroom. It should be a *wave* of success. The waters have already been tested so all you have to do is jump in (feet first)!

INVITES

What You Need:

* colored construction paper
* scissors
* colored markers

What You Do:

1. Cut out fish shapes—or anything else that says beach party to you—from construction paper. Make sure your invites are large enough to write on, but small enough to fit in envelopes.

2. On the front of your invite, write something like, "It's an all-night beach party…" Then flip it over and write, "…in my room (or living room or wherever)!"

3. Fill out all the party details on the back. Don't forget to mention that your guests should pack a sleeping bag, PJ's, and whatever else you want them to bring.

DÉCOR

String patio lights around the party room. Set out beach chairs, beach umbrellas, beach towels, and beach balls. Get a mini plastic or inflatable wading pool at a discount store (or borrow one from your neighbor, who has a one) and fill it with about a half inch of water. Throw in a few seashells, and place some buckets and shovels around the room. As for music, it's all about reggae.

Limbo

This is a favorite game at beach parties. See if your friends can defy all laws of physics by twisting their bodies into backbends and other amazing shapes.

How to Play:

1. Have two volunteers, one on each side, hold each end of a five-foot-long pole (or a long broom or something) at about shoulder height.

2. Crank up the reggae music and have your friends stand in line. One at a time, each guest should try to walk under the pole by bending backward—not by bending forward and not by crouching. Anyone who bends forward or crouches is eliminated. Anyone who knocks down the pole is also eliminated.

3. Once everyone in line has had a turn, have the volunteers move the pole down a notch to chest level. Have everyone give it another go, again eliminating those who don't make the cut. Keep going, moving the pole down a few inches at each turn.

4. The last person to be left in the game is the grand champion and should be crowned as such.

Beached Mermaids

Step into your sleeping bag standing up, and pull it tight around your waist. You'll feel just like a mermaid—sort of.

How to Play:

1. Have your guests line up on one side of the room, standing inside their sleeping bags.

2. When you yell "Go!" the "mermaids" should maneuver themselves to the other side of the room any way they can—hopping, rolling, scooting, wriggling, somersaulting, waddling—without removing their sleeping bags.

3. The first one to make it to the other side of the room and back is the winner.

Sandscapes

Make sand art projects for your friends to take home from the party. They make great decorations for your dresser, too.

What You Need:

- ❋ empty baby food jars, or other small, clear containers
- ❋ several different colors of sand (from craft stores)
- ❋ small funnels
- ❋ small scoops (like the kind that come in coffee cans)

What You Do:

1. Place each color of sand in a separate clear, plastic container or jar.

2. Place a funnel in the opening of the jar that you're using to hold your sandscape. Scoop sand into the funnel and filter it into the jar.

3. Alternate layers of colors until your jar is filled to the top. Put the lid on securely.

Note: *Get creative with designs! Make diagonal layers by tilting your jar as you pour sand in. Or, make the colored layers vary in thickness.*

Ankle Twist

If you're going to be barefoot on the beach (or in the bedroom), there's no better accessory than an ankle bracelet. Try this one—it's a little bit tricky. Make sure you hold on tightly while twisting!

What You Need:

- ❋ embroidery floss in different colors
- ❋ scissors
- ❋ ruler
- ❋ tape

What You Do:

Step 1

1. Cut five different colored pieces of embroidery floss each into a 3-foot length. Tie them together in a knot three inches from one end. Use tape to fasten the end to your work surface.

2. Gather the strings together as a group and twist them together tightly! Keep twisting in the same direction until you have a tight length.

3. Hold the length taut with one hand. Use a finger from the other hand to press into the center of it.

4. Fold the length in half by bringing the end of the string you're holding to meet the taped end with the knot. Carefully take your finger away. The twisted length should now spin around by itself! Remove the tape but keep holding the ends.

Step 4

Step 5

5. Tie the twisty bracelet around your ankle, then carefully cut off any excess floss. Beautiful!

Beach Braids

Some girls will just want a couple of braids on one side of their head. And some might want all of their hair braided.

What You Need:

* several small beads in different colors

* aluminum foil (cut into 1-inch squares)

What You Do:

1. Grasp a small lock of hair at the hairline or the base of the neck.

2. Separate the lock into three tiny strands. Braid from the scalp to the end of the strands.

3. Take a square of aluminum foil and wrap it tightly around the end of the braid.

4. Slip two or three beads over the foil and onto the end of the braid.

5. Bend the end of the foil into a clump until the beads are secure.

EATS

You can really work up an appetite after a day at the beach.

Sloppy Honey Joes

makes 8

Make the day before and reheat.

What You Need:

* 2-1/2 pounds lean ground beef
* 1 large onion, chopped
* 1 clove garlic, minced
* 1 cup ketchup
* 1/4 cup honey
* 1 tablespoon chili powder
* 1 tablespoon mustard

* 1/2 teaspoon salt
* 8 hamburger rolls
* measuring cups and spoons
* large pot
* wooden spoon
* an adult to help

What You Do:

1. Ask an adult to help brown the ground beef over medium heat in a large pot. Add the onion and garlic, and cook until they're soft—for about 5 minutes. Drain.

2. Add the ketchup, honey, chili powder, mustard, and salt, and bring the mixture to a boil. Reduce heat to low, and simmer for about 15 minutes. Stir occasionally with a wooden spoon. Sauce will thicken as it cooks down.

3. Serve the meat mixture on rolls.

Sweet Potato Fries

serves 8

What You Need:

* 4 large sweet potatoes
* 1 tablespoon olive oil
* salt, to taste
* measuring spoons

* knife (and an adult to help with cutting)
* bowl
* baking sheet

What You Do:

1. Preheat oven to 400°.

2. Ask an adult to peel the sweet potatoes, and then cut them in half lengthwise. Then, cut each half in half again twice—so you end up with 16 wedges.

3. Toss wedges in a bowl and coat with the olive oil.

4. Spread out the wedges on a baking sheet. Sprinkle with salt.

5. Bake for 30 minutes or until the edges are browned. Serve right away while still crispy and warm.

Fruit Kabobs

make on party day

What You Need:

* fruit (kiwi, pineapple, orange sections, grapes, melon, papaya)
* 2 limes
* wooden skewers
* serving platter

* knife
* plastic wrap
* decorative flowers (optional)
* an adult to help

What You Do:

1. Allow enough time to cut the fruit. Wash, dry, and peel the fruit as needed. Cut into 1-inch pieces. Make sure that fragile fruit such as kiwi and papaya are cut thick enough so they stay on the kabobs. Cut the limes into wedges.

2. Arrange the cut fruit in different combos on the skewers. Lay the kabobs on a round platter so the ends are around the edge of the circle and the pointed parts meet in the middle.

   Place the lime wedges around the outside of the platter for garnish. If you have one, place a decorative flower in the middle of the platter. Cover with plastic wrap and refrigerate until serving time.

Extra Slumber Party Themes

Looking to do something different at your sleepover bash? Here are some other quick and cute ideas:

Bon Voyage Bash: Have a bud who's shoving off for the summer or moving away? Then this party theme is perfect! Think sailboats, think life preservers, think friend*ships*. It doesn't have to be a going away party full of tissues and tears—it can be fun, too—full of hugs and laughs. Make some yummy food, play your fave games, and don't forget going-away gifts! Here are a couple of ideas if you're struggling to come up with a gift for your bud:

✻ Colorful pre-paid long distance calling cards.

✻ Stationery.

✻ Cool commemorative stamps.

✻ A pretty pen.

✻ A disposable camera so she can send pictures of her new pad.

✻ Have everyone address pre-stamped postcards or envelopes so all your faraway friend has to do to drop a line is add her update and pop it in the mail.

✻ Create a Ship's Log by decorating a small address book with stickers. Write "Ship's Log" on the front of it. Have your friends sign in their names, addresses, phone numbers, and e-mail as they arrive at your party. When the party's over, present the filled address book as a present to the guest of honor. She'll have no excuse for not staying in touch!

So-Long Summer Bash: Take advantage of the outdoors and throw a bash before you have to get back to the books! Have your folks fire up the barbeque for some burgers and hotdogs (and don't forget tasty cold treats for dessert, but keep them out of the heat!), and play these ridiculous relays:

✻ *Ankle Grab:* Each player bends forward and grabs her own ankles. In that position, players go to the finish line and back.

✻ *Glacier Melt:* Teams must try to melt an ice cube while passing it from player to player. Whichever team completely melts their ice cube first wins. No fair using your mouth!

✻ *Bubblegum Blowout:* The first player sticks three pieces of gum in their mouth, recites "Pledge of Allegiance," and blows a bubble before tagging the next player.

✻ *Potato Carry:* The first player walks to the finish line, balancing one potato on each hand—knuckles up, arms out like a zombie.

Chapter 5

Best Birthday Bashes

Your birthday is coming up? Hey, you were *born* to party! And throwing an awesome birthday bash is a *piece of cake*—all it takes is a little creativity.

MAKE IT INVITING

When making invitations, you can't go wrong with construction paper, markers, glitter, and glue. But why not try something new? Here's an idea: Blow up a balloon, but don't knot it. Instead, pinch the end so no air gets out. Then, using a marker, *carefully* (so the balloon doesn't pop!) write the party info on it. Let the air out, and stick the deflated balloon in an envelope. Repeat for everyone on your guest list! Your friends will have to blow up the balloons to get your party scoop.

As a safety precaution, before you seal the envelopes and mail the balloons, also write the party info on a slip of paper, fold it up very small, and put it inside each deflated balloon. So if a balloon pops, your pals will still have the party details!

What's a Birthday Party without a Piñata?

You can buy a piñata at just about any party supplies store, but making one is so much more fun. Here's how....

What You Need:

* newspaper
* balloon
* ruler
* 1 foot of string
* scissors
* tape
* 1/2 cup flour
* 3 cups warm water

* colored tissue paper
* pin
* large bowl
* measuring cups
* fun stuff to fill the piñata
* plastic bat or yardstick
* blindfold

What You Do:

1. Cover your work surface with newspaper (don't use all of it—you'll need to have plenty left for making your piñata).

2. Blow up the balloon, and knot it closed.

3. Measure and cut a 1-foot piece of string, fold it in half, and securely tape the ends to the top of the balloon (this should make a loop and will be used for hanging your finished piñata).

Step 3

4. Make a paste by mixing 1/2 cup flour with 3 cups warm water in a large bowl. Mix thoroughly. It shouldn't be clumpy or runny—just sticky. If it's too thick, add more water. Too thin? Add flour.

5. Cut or tear the rest of your newspaper into strips. Dip the strips into the flour paste and place the strips one at a time over the balloon's surface until the balloon is completely covered. Be sure not to cover your string (except where it's taped), and leave a small opening at the opposite end of the balloon (this is where you'll insert the piñata prizes!). Let it dry completely.

Step 5

6. Cover the balloon with two more layers of newspaper strips, letting them dry between each layer. Try to place strips in criss-crossing directions each time.

7. Once all the newspaper layers are dry, cut out squares of tissue paper and glue them onto your piñata, too—in enough layers so you can't see the newspaper through it. Use a color scheme or make a design. For example, use yellow and black tissue paper to form a smiley face. Or just make rainbow stripes. Whatever suits your fancy. Let it dry.

8. Stick a pin in the piñata's opening to pop the balloon, and then fill the piñata with lots of little goodies— candies, gum, costume jewelry, party favors, or other fun stuff.

9. Cover the opening by gluing on several pieces of tissue paper. Let it dry before hanging.

10. Ready to get the goodies? One by one, hand your guests a plastic bat or yardstick. Blindfold each guest one at a time, twirl her around a few times, and let her take three swings. Continue letting everyone try until someone breaks the piñata. Everyone can share the treats inside, but you might want to have a special little prize set aside for the person who breaks the piñata!

Step 10

THAT TAKES THE CAKE

You simply can't have a birthday party without cake and ice cream. Store-bought cakes can be perfectly yummy, and so can the ones you make from a box. But rather than making the routine 8-inch round cake, try this fun variation. It's cake, but it looks like ice cream! In cones!

Cupcake Cones

serves 24

What You Need:

* 1 box cake mix (and the ingredients it requires)
* 2 12-packs of ice cream cones (with flat bottoms)
* 1 can frosting
* colorful sprinkles
* measuring cups and spoons
* bowl
* mixing spoons
* muffin pans (each with 12 cups)

What You Do:

1. In a bowl, mix the cake batter according to the package directions.
2. Place one ice cream cone upright in each cup of a muffin pan.
3. Pour the prepared cake mix into each cone, filling to just over the lip at the middle part of the cone.
4. Bake according to cupcake directions on the cake mix box.
5. Let cupcake cones cool. Frost, and decorate with sprinkles.

DREAMY ICE CREAM

And the perfect go-with for your Cupcake Cones? Ice cream, of course! For custom-blended ice cream, stock up on plenty of vanilla, chocolate and strawberry, and then let your guests toss in their own add-ins, such as candy or cookie pieces. Making custom flavors is easy if you let the ice cream sit out for a few minutes before scooping. Then, just spoon the ice cream into a bowl, add your toppings of choice, and stir until it's as soft and mixed as you like. Here are some suggestions for yummy stuff to stir into your ice cream....

Chocolate Chips: Add mini chocolate chips (as many as you like) to chocolate or vanilla ice cream.

Fruit Fiesta: Add your favorite fruit to vanilla ice cream or any flavor sherbert. You can use fresh fruit or fruit from a can (drain the juice before adding).

Cookie Cream: Crush your favorite kind of cookies into bite-size pieces and sprinkle them over vanilla, chocolate, or mint ice cream.

Candy Bar: Your favorite munchies are M&M's, Snickers, Reese's Pieces, or Heath Bars? Smash 'em up, and throw them into your ice cream (whatever flavor you choose).

READY, SET, BLOW

Here's a tip for blowing out all those birthday candles so you're sure to get your wish. As soon as everyone is on that last refrain of "Happy Birthday," lower your face to cake level. Take the deepest breath you can, pucker up your lips, and blow while slightly moving your head from side to side (like you're shaking your head "no"). The candles won't go out as easily if you stand above them and blow down on them.

BIRTHDAY BASH THEMES

Where to throw a b-day fling? Follow your personality. You're a totally sporty, active gal? Have your party at the batting cages, bowling alley, or skating rink. You love to read your horoscope? Plan a Look-Into-the-Future Fest. You'd rather read mystery stories? Have a Whodunnit? Party. Read on about some fun party themes.

LOOK-INTO-THE-FUTURE FEST

Plan the whole party around the future, cool fortunes and all.

Invites

Trace your hand onto a colored piece of paper, and cut out the shape. Draw a few lines on the palm and write something catchy like, "I see an awesome party in your future." On the back, write all the necessary party details. For extra laughs, ask all your guests to dress in outfits they predict will be super fashionable in the future.

Décor

Hang tons of purple, blue, and gray streamers in the door frame that leads to the party room. Cut out moons and stars in different sizes from colored construction paper, and hang them from the ceiling using fishing line and clear tape. The clear line will make it look like the stars are hanging in midair. Shut off the main lights, and turn on colored night lights for a pretty, glowing effect.

To Do

Fortune Cards: Start with a deck of cards. For each guest, pull out one playing card. On the solid-colored or patterned backs of the cards, place a label with an upbeat handwritten fortune such as, "You are about to come into tons of money." Spread the cards face up (fortunes down) on a table, and have each girl pick one from the pile (don't peek). Once everyone has her card, flip them over to read the fortunes. No trading.

Guessing Game: Write down several questions you think your friends would be able to answer about each other. They might be about favorite TV shows, celebs of choice, favorite desserts, most hated songs, and least likely outfits worn. Then throw the questions into an old hat or a bowl. Pair off your friends, and give one person in each pair a slip of paper and a pen. The person who has the paper will be trying to predict how the other girl might answer her questions. An example would be, "What is the one TV show your bud stays home every week to watch?" You should ask the questions, and give the girls who have the paper a few minutes to write down an answer (no giving each other clues!). Once everyone has written down an answer, the other girls, one at a time, say out loud what their answers are ("My favorite TV show is…"). The person who accurately answers the most questions about her partner wins. After that, have the guessers and the answerers switch roles.

Cake

Decorate a frosted cake with candy stars, and align birthday candles in the shape of a crescent moon. If you're an ambitious cake decorator, draw your zodiac sign in pretty icing gels.

WHODUNNIT? PARTY

It's mystery madness—a party filled with codes, clues, and tons of case-cracking.

Invites

Fold a piece of colored paper in half and draw a big question mark on the front. Then place your fingerprints everywhere by pressing your thumb first on an ink pad, and then pressing it down on the invitation. Use all different colors of ink. Inside, write "To find out whodunnit, show up at my house," and then write down the necessary party info in backward letters.

ƎЯ'UOY
ᗡƎTIVИI

АᗺↃᗡƎᖷᎻⅠႱꓘⅬM
ИOꟼᏢᖉƧTUѴWXYƧ

Décor

Get several rolls of yellow streamers and string them around the party room (but do not twist—this is supposed to look like crime-scene tape). Take a thick black permanent marker and write on the streamers: "Police Line—Do Not Cross." Also, take a large pair of shoes and trace around them to make shoe prints on pieces of construction paper. Cut out the shoe prints and tape them to the floor, making suspicious tracks around the party room.

To Do

Get a Clue: As each guest arrives, give her a bag containing a small plastic magnifying glass, pad of paper, pen, and handmade detective badge. Also include an index card with "CLUE" written in big letters on one side—on the flip side include a clue about a certain location in the house. For example, "Underneath that which gives us water" for the kitchen sink. Hide small treats or puzzles in each clue location, and have guests track them all down.

Police Report: Choose someone everyone will know (a teacher, for example) but don't tell who you've picked. Once everyone has a pad of paper and a pen, you should read a description of the "suspect" aloud. Describe the suspect's features and characteristics. While you read off the details, each guest should do a composite drawing on paper, sketching her version of the suspect. When everybody's finished, see if they can guess who the suspect is. If no one does, tell them and watch everybody laugh as they check out one another's sketches.

Gotcha!: For each party member, assign an easy-to-spot object, such as an apple or a hat, in the room. Then announce that a criminal is in search of that object and will be showing up intermittently during the party to try to steal it. Have family members travel in and out of the room at different times throughout the party and attempt to remove an object without the guests catching them. (And don't shout out about other people's objects being stolen—each guest is responsible for her own.) Anytime the thief gets away, the person responsible for the stolen object is out of the game. The last person not to have her stuff thieved is the winner.

Cake

Using icings and gels, write the name of each guest on individual cupcakes—but with a twist. Write the letters backward (sample alphabet on page 65), and leave them on the table so everyone will have to figure out whose cupcake is whose.

GIFTED AND GRATEFUL

Everyone loves watching the birthday gal tear open her gifts, especially when you're the giver. Have a party basket handy in the corner of the room to hold the presents when your friends come in. That way, no gift will be ignored or overlooked. When it's time for the grand opening, have everyone gather around and make sure to thank each guest after you open her gift—even if she gives you a chartreuse T-shirt you wouldn't want to dry dishes with! Have your BFF keep a list of who gave you what as you open the presents, so you can be sure you don't get mixed up when trying to keep the gift-givers straight later on. That way, too, you can be sure to send gift-appropriate thank-you notes later.

Saving Face

No matter what gift you receive, always find at least one positive thing to say about it. If you get a gift you don't like, don't let it show on your face. Accept it graciously, and always be sure to say, "Thank you!"

"But how can I honestly say thank you when I really don't like the present?" you might ask. Well, you can say it creatively instead. If you can't bring yourself to be enthusiastic about the purple-sequined bracelets and belt, acknowledge the gesture instead: "Oh, you always find the most interesting and unique gifts! Thank you so much!"

Present and Accounted For

It's not your birthday, but you've been invited to the b-day party of the year. What to give as the perfect, extra creative gift? Here are a few original ideas with a twist....

* *A gift certificate:* No, not another $20 to spend at the local music store! Give the gift of your undivided attention. Help your bud with fractions. Or, maybe she'd love to get her hair whipped into an updo by you. Not only are you giving a gift that no one else can give, but you don't have to spend a dime! Bonus.

* *An endangered species:* Know someone who'd want nothing more than a whale of a gift? Surf the Internet and check out any number of great animal adoption programs out there. Your friend will be the only girl in school who has her own manatee!

* *A collage or photo album:* Gather some favorite snaps of your friend and the gang, and make an extra personal photo album or collage. Be sure to jot down names and any key phrases that will make the memories come alive ("Who knew that waiter really was French!"). This is a great project for a bunch of friends to do together.

* *One more idea:* Shopping at dollar stores can be fun. Look for cute candles, fun stickers, cool pens and pencils, little stuffed animals, sachets, and mini bath products. Instead of blowing money on one big thing, why not make a special gift basket filled with lots of little goodies? Sometimes getting lots of little stuff is more fun than one big gift.

Why Thank You?

Wondering why you have to send thank-you cards when you're already thanking your guests in person the day of the party? There are two very sound reasons for sending thank-you notes.

The first reason is the most important because it is part of the foundation of friendship. Relationships are most enduring and rewarding when each person contributes equally to the mix. When one person is always a taker, or a giver, resentment often follows and the friendship might not last long.

So when a friend or relative remembers a special occasion—goes to the trouble and expense of choosing, buying (or creating), and wrapping a gift—a spoken thank-you, however heartfelt, doesn't quite equal the effort made by the giver. Your trouble in writing and sending a note evens things up a bit.

The second reason is very practical. Showing appreciation in a special way is remembered the next time gift-giving occasions come around.

Having trouble putting your thank-you thoughts on paper? Here is an easy way to accomplish the task in five minutes flat:

"Dear (name), What a wonderful (name the gift)! I love it, and I will think of you every time I (use, eat, wear) it. You are always so (original, creative, kind, thoughtful, generous). Thanks for remembering me on my birthday." Add a personal note ("See you at the football game!" "You're always a wonderful friend!"). Then, sign, address, stamp, send it, and you're done!

Chapter 6

Happy Holiday Celebrations

While we firmly believe that any time is a good time for a party, holidays like Christmas, Hanukkah, New Year's, Valentine's Day, and Halloween are perfect times to go all out and have fun with a bunch of your friends. You know how that old saying goes: The more, the merrier!

A SUGAR -'N' -SPICE SOIRÉE

Oh, the weather outside is frightful, and what could be more delightful... than a holiday cookie party! When the blustering wind and swirling snowflakes make sledding and building snowgirls feel like work, ditch your icy mittens and spend the afternoon by a warm stove, sipping hot chocolate and munching on warm cookies. Invite your best pals over for a holiday cookie party and recipe exchange!

GINGERBREAD PERSON INVITES

What You Need:

* large gingerbread cookie cutters (or stars for Hanukkah)
* pens and markers
* construction paper in green and red (or blue and white for Hanukkah, or any other two colors you like)
* scissors
* spray glue
* gold (for Christmas or Kwanzaa) or silver glitter (for Hanukkah)
* hole puncher
* ribbon
* envelopes big enough to hold the invites

What You Do:

1. To make each invite, start by tracing a large gingerbread man (or star) cookie cutter onto your green (or blue or whatever) construction paper.

2. Then, trace a gingerbread lady (use the same cookie cutter) on the red (or white or whatever) construction paper.

3. Cut out both shapes with scissors.

4. If you are making gingerbread people, use a black marker to add a bow tie, hat, or mustache to your cutout man. Pen in all the necessary party details.

5. On the red (or white or whatever) construction paper, create a party partner for your jolly gingerbread man by drawing on eyelashes, a blouse and accessories. To create a skirt, cut out a small skirt shape from construction paper and spray glue to the back of it to attach. On your gingerbread lady, write "Recipe," and instruct each guest to write down her favorite holiday cookie creation and bring it to the party for a recipe exchange.

6. Spray some glue on the blank areas of your gingerbread pair (or your stars) and bedazzle them with gold (or silver) glitter.

7. Using the hole puncher, punch a small hole in both cutouts, and then tie 'em together with ribbon.

8. Use pens and markers to decorate your envelopes with Christmas trees, dreidels, or whatever else you like. You can also jazz them up with stickers and more glitter!

DÉCOR

The focus of your cookie party is (no surprise!) your kitchen. So why not adorn the kitchen walls with colored lights and colorful gingerbread man garlands?

Colorful Gingerbread Man Garlands

What You Need:

* construction paper in any two colors you like
* small gingerbread cookie cutters (or stars or circles for Hanukkah)
* pencil
* scissors
* removable tape
* hole pucher
* ribbon

What You Do:

1. Take some colored construction paper and fold it back and forth into accordion folds (make sure your folds all line up into one neat stack). The size between folds is up to you, but needs to be wide enough to fit your small cookie cutter.

2. Place your small cookie cutter on top of the folded paper, trace it, and cut out the shape. But make sure to leave the fold uncut at the hands—that's how the cutouts stay linked. Now unfold and voilà!

3. Lengthen your garland by connecting each colored strand with removable tape at the end. Deck the whole room! Just punch holes in the tops of their little heads and string with ribbons, or use removable tape to stick them directly on the wall.

Even easier? Construction paper chains. Take strips of colored paper that are 2 inches wide and 5 inches long. Bend one strip into a circle, and close the ends with removable tape. Slip a second strip through the ring and tape the ends. Repeat. Soon, you'll have a string of holiday color.

Another decorating idea (the simplest yet!): Tie silver ribbon to holiday shaped cookie cutters and dangle them above windows and door frames like ornaments!

You'll need to be fully stocked for your holiday bake-off, so make sure you have plenty of cookie cutters, at least four baking sheets, some cookie cooling racks, and a couple of rolling pins. And clear lots of room! Elbows fly when the rollin' gets goin', so be sure to have plenty of working space.

And you can't have a cookie party without holiday music, so dig through your family's collection for fun classics, hit the record store for a few new festive CD's to add to your collection, or tune the radio to the station that's playing holiday hits!

To Make Sure Your Cookie Party Doesn't Crumble:

• Consider mixing the dough in advance so that once everyone arrives, you can get right to work.

• Chill the dough for at least two hours (or overnight) before rolling. Have a flour canister handy for dusting, because dough can be very sticky (flour absorbs some of the stickiness).

• Don't forget to preheat. Turn on the oven 10 to 15 minutes before baking so that it will be at the right temperature when you start. Plan on baking two trays of cookies at a time, rotating them halfway through cooking (this helps to ensure that all the cookies are evenly baked).

• You might want to bake some batches in advance, so there'll be plenty of extras for each guest to take home!

EATS

Time to make the cookies...and munch 'em warm out of the oven! Offer dunk-worthy drinks to go with your fresh-from-the-oven cookies. Milk does a cookie good, but it's great to serve hot drinks as well. Whip up some winter favorites like hot chocolate and hot apple cider (just simmer cider on a stove top until hot, pour into a mug, and garnish with cinnamon sticks or sprinkle with ground cinnamon).

Sugar Cookies

makes 36

What You Need:

* 1 cup sugar
* 1/2 cup butter
* 1 egg
* 3 tablespoons cream
* 2-1/4 cups flour
* 1 teaspoon baking powder
* colored crystals
* measuring cups and spoons

* large bowl
* wooden spoon
* small bowl
* rolling pin
* waxed paper
* spatula
* cookie sheet
* cookie cutters

What You Do:

1. In a large bowl, beat together the sugar and butter with a wooden spoon, until creamy. Add the egg and the cream. Mix well.

2. In a small bowl, mix the flour and the baking powder.

3. Gradually, add the flour mixture from the small bowl to the mixture in the large bowl, stirring well. If the dough seems too sticky, add a little more flour.

4. Divide the dough into two balls. Place each dough ball between two sheets of waxed paper. Flatten each ball with the rolling pin. Chill the dough in the refrigerator for several hours or overnight.

5. When the dough is chilled, remove the waxed paper. Sprinkle flour on the work surface, rolling pin, and dough. Flatten dough with the rolling pin again, and use cookie cutters to create shapes.

6. Use a spatula to place the cookies on an ungreased cookie sheet, and decorate with colored crystals.

7. Bake at 350° for about 12 to 15 minutes, until light, golden brown. Repeat with any unused dough scraps.

8. Remove the cookies from the oven, and let cool.

Gingerbread Cookies

makes 24

What You Need:

* 1 cup sugar
* 1/2 cup butter
* 1 cup molasses
* 2-1/4 cups flour
* 1/2 teaspoon baking soda
* 2 tablespoons ginger
* 1 teaspoon cinnamon

* measuring cups and spoons
* large bowl
* wooden spoon
* small bowl
* rolling pin
* cookie cutters
* cookie sheet

What You Do:

1. In a large bowl, beat together the sugar and butter. Mix in the molasses.

2. In a small bowl, combine the flour, baking soda, ginger, and cinnamon.

3. Gradually, add the flour mixture from the small bowl to the mixture in the large bowl, stirring well. If the dough seems too sticky, add a little more flour.

4. Chill the dough in the refrigerator for easier handling (two hours to overnight).

5. When the dough is chilled, flour your work surface and the rolling pin, and roll the dough out into a thin sheet.

6. Cut out the cookies with the cookie cutters and bake at 350° for about 10 to 12 minutes on an ungreased cookie sheet. Repeat with any unused dough scraps.

7. Remove the cookies from the oven, and let cool completely before decorating with colored frosting (recipe follows).

Colored Frosting

makes plenty to frost a batch of cookies

What You Need:

* 3 cups confectioners' sugar
* 2 tablespoons milk
* 1-1/2 tablespoons fresh lemon juice
* food coloring

* measuring cups and spoons
* bowl
* wooden spoon
* several small bowls

What You Do:

1. Mix the sugar, milk, and lemon juice in a bowl until smooth. If the mixture is too thick, add a little more milk.

2. Divide the frosting into several small bowls, and add food coloring a few drops at a time until each bowl reaches the desired shade.

M & M's Cookies

What You Need:

* 2-1/2 cups flour
* 1/2 teaspoon baking soda
* 1/2 teaspoon salt
* 1 cup butter, softened
* 3/4 cup sugar
* 3/4 cup packed brown sugar
* 2 eggs
* 1 teaspoon vanilla extract
* 1 cup chopped pecans

* 1-1/2 cups of chopped holiday-colored M&M's, plus 1 cup of whole candies
* measuring cups and spoons
* teaspoons
* small bowl
* large bowl
* wooden spoon
* greased cookie sheet

What You Do:

1. In a small bowl, combine the flour, baking soda, and salt.

2. In a large bowl, beat together the butter and both sugars until light and fluffy. Add the eggs and vanilla extract. Then, gradually beat in the flour mixture from the small bowl. Add the chopped nuts and chopped candies.

3. Taking chunks at a time, round each chunk of dough into a ball, using teaspoons or your hands, and drop each one onto the greased cookie sheet. Flatten each ball a little.

4. Bake at 350° for about 6 to 7 minutes.

5. Remove from the oven, and add several whole M&M's to the top of each cookie. Return to the oven, and bake again for 3 to 5 minutes.

TO DO

While the aroma of baking cookies wafts through the house, rinse the flour from your hands and trade in your aprons for smocks. After all, what's a party without favors?

Paint a Recipe Box: Every new cookie baker needs a recipe box in which to store her savory secrets! Most craft stores carry plain wooden recipe boxes for painting and decorating. Give each girl a plain box and then make it a party activity to customize it with paints, glitter, buttons...even flat kitchen magnets!

After you are finished decorating, get out the recipes that you asked each friend to bring and place them in the center of your worktable. Provide a pile of index cards and plenty of pens so that each girl can copy the recipes she likes. Now you and your buds can copy and trade each other's faves to fill your boxes (once their paint has dried, of course)!

Brown Bag It: Let your cooks create their own decorative cookie totes. Start with small, brown-handled shopping bags or lunch bags. Using clean cookie cutters as outlines, cut sponges into holiday shapes. Dip one side of each sponge into shallow bowls of paint and stamp designs on the outside of each bag. Stuff colored tissue inside the bags, and fill them with your delicious homemade cookies! These bags make a great re-gift, too— but don't wait more than a day to give your favorite bud (or perhaps a friend who didn't make it to your cookie get-together) that delicious bag of homemade treats.

Tree Candy: Make edible ornaments—no dough needed. Gather up metal cookie cutters and lots of different flavors of Jolly Rancher candies. Remove the wrappers on each candy. You can use one color for each ornament, or combine colors to make the ornaments bold and bright.

Coat the metal cookie cutters with non-stick cooking spray, and then place them on baking trays. Place a few Jolly Ranchers inside each cookie cutter and bake at 350° until melted. Let them cool slightly, then have an adult carefully remove the melted Jolly Ranchers from the cookie cutters. While the candy is still a little warm and gummy, use toothpicks to make holes at the tops so you can string ribbon through the holes and hang the candy ornaments. They're both cute *and* edible!

Bring Home the Dough: Give your guests one last take-home treat—dough logs! They can slice 'em and bake 'em at home.

Spice up the traditional sugar cookie recipe on page 75 with sweet surprises. Divide the dough into four bowls, then form each quarter into a log shape. Roll each log in colored sprinkles, sugar crystals, cinnamon, or finely crushed candy bars until the outside is coated. Wrap each dough log in colored cellophane, gathered and tied with ribbon on each end. Remember to attach baking info. Your buds can take the logs home to refrigerate or freeze for later. When they want yummy cookies, they can just thaw, slice, and bake! Sugar cookie dough logs also make great gifts to take to all the other holiday parties you're invited to.

HALLOWEEN SCREAM!

No *bones* about it—Halloween is a time for *monster* partying. Ghosts and spiders dangle in windows everywhere. Scarecrows and pumpkins perch on front porches, and you and your friends are decked out in your costumes. It's time to throw a spell-binding monster bash!

INVITES

Your buds will go batty for these simply spooky invites. Summon the ghouls on your guest list to your spook-tacular soirée with glittery, handmade ghost invites. BOO!

What You Need:

* white construction paper
* pencil
* scissors
* fine-point black pen
* spray glue
* silver glitter

* some googly eyes (don't forget you'll need two eyes for each invite)
* tacky glue
* silver paint-pen
* black envelopes
* Halloween stickers

What You Do:

1. Fold a piece of white construction paper in half the short way. Place the paper width-wise on a smooth surface so the fold is at the top.

2. With a pencil, sketch a simple ghost-like shape, with its head at that top, folded edge.

3. Cut out the ghost, only don't cut off that folded edge because you want your invites to flip open at the top to reveal your haunted party details.

4. After you've cut out the first ghost, use it as a pattern to trace and cut out the rest of your invites.

5. Use a black fine-point pen to write the party info inside each ghost.

6. On the front of each ghost, lightly spray some glue and then sprinkle on a thin layer of silver glitter.

7. Once the glitter has set and dried, dab each googly eye with a bit of tacky glue and carefully press it down in place.

8. Let the invites dry completely, preferably overnight.

9. Using a silver paint-pen, address each envelope (preferably black), and then insert the invites.

10. Decorate envelopes with spooky Halloween stickers! Then, stamp 'em and put those scary things in the mail.

DÉCOR

Party stores have tons of great stuff you can get for cheap in order to decorate your party perfectly. You should be able to find most of the stuff for the following ideas at one.

Start by dangling plastic bats from the ceiling of the party room using fishing line. For an awesome effect, hang them by a window or a fan to make them gently sway with the breeze. To set a spooky mood, get black lightbulbs (they make everything that's white glow).

Next get glow-in-the-dark paint at an art supplies store and paint eyes on black construction paper. Cut out the eye shapes and tape them on the walls of your party room. Your guests will suspect lurking monsters are gazing out at them!

Buy black and orange helium balloons and have the party store cut the strings so they are long enough to brush your guests' faces as they enter the dark party room (and when the lights go back on, they make for a festive, cobwebby feel). Play a tape of spooky sounds (record these ahead of time: scary howling, squeaky doors, cats meowing, and haunted screams).

To make a giant spider, blow up two black balloons, tie the ends together, and tape the tied balloon ends to the center of the ceiling. Then tape eight black streamers to the ceiling, right where you taped the balloons, and ending the streamers at the far edges of the room. The idea is to let the streamers droop slightly so they look like spooky spider legs! To add spiderwebs, bunch cotton balls together and pull fibers apart slowly until they are web-like—spray with hair spray to stiffen and tape onto party room corners (you can also buy "spiderwebs" at the party store).

TO DO

Let the fun begin the minute your guests walk through the door. Set out bowls of candy corn, small orange gumdrops, and black Jujy Fruits. Your buds can use sturdy thread and craft needles (the dull, large ones) to string these edible jewels into necklaces and bracelets. The trick is to string more jewels than you eat! Once everyone has arrived, gather up your guests for some ghoulish games.

Witch's Broom Pumpkin Push: You can't help but get swept up in the spirit of this game. Play it inside if you have a large, clear room; outside if the weather is OK.

Start by dividing your ghosts—oops, we mean *guests*—into equal teams. Each team will need a miniature pumpkin (or a blown-up balloon, but have plenty of extra balloons if you're playing outside because they'll easily blow away) and a broom. Choose a starting point and mark a goal line 20 to 40 feet away. At a signal, the first person on each team sweeps the pumpkins to the end goal and back. Then, she hands the broom to the next team member and it's the second person's turn. The first team to have every player complete the course has the last cackle!

Mummy Madness: Here's a fun way to get your guests under wraps! Divide your buds into two-person teams and give each team a roll of toilet paper. One member of the team is the mummy, and the other will costume her. At the signal, the girl acting as the mummy must stand very still, hands at her sides, as her teammate quickly and carefully wraps her from head to toe in toilet paper. Then switch roles and repeat. (But don't forget to unwrap the original mummy first.) The first team to wrap both players wins. Victory moaning required!

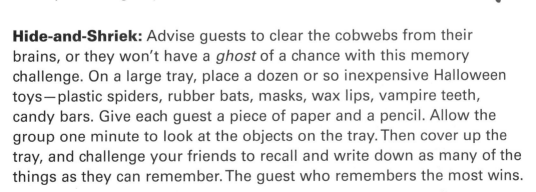

Hide-and-Shriek: Advise guests to clear the cobwebs from their brains, or they won't have a *ghost* of a chance with this memory challenge. On a large tray, place a dozen or so inexpensive Halloween toys—plastic spiders, rubber bats, masks, wax lips, vampire teeth, candy bars. Give each guest a piece of paper and a pencil. Allow the group one minute to look at the objects on the tray. Then cover up the tray, and challenge your friends to recall and write down as many of the things as they can remember. The guest who remembers the most wins.

Boo Are You?: On index cards, write down Halloween creatures—ghost, witch, cat, owl, werewolf, vampire, bat, mummy. Pick one person in your party to be It and blindfold her. Everyone else receives an index card. Players stand in a circle around It. She twirls around, stops in front of a person, and asks, "Boo are you?" The player answers in the voice of the creature on her card. A bat might squeak, a cat meow, a witch cackle, a werewolf howl, an owl hoot. If It guesses the identity of the person, that person becomes It and everyone in the circle trades cards. Otherwise, It goes on and talks to another creature. If you think you're too old for this game, you're not!

EATS

Treats for gobblin' have to be sweet!

Rest-in-Peace Pops

makes 12

Conjure these up ahead of time. Keep frozen until ready to serve.

What You Need:

* 1 quart chocolate ice cream
* 1 quart mint ice cream
* crushed chocolate cookie crumbs
* gummy worms
* 12 5-ounce paper cups
* 12 plastic novelty tombstones (in the cake decoration section of party stores)
* ice-cream scooper or large serving spoon
* 12 wooden Popsicle sticks

What You Do:

1. Let both flavors of ice cream soften slightly. Put a tombstone face down in the bottom of each paper cup.

2. Sprinkle a layer of cookie crumbs on top of the tombstones as "dirt."

3. Then add the first layer ice cream in each cup.

4. Stick a gummy worm or two into the first layer of ice cream, so it looks like they are coming out of the dirt.

5. Then, add a second layer of ice cream. You should begin alternating flavors until you reach the top of the cup. Make the layers as thick or thin as you want.

6. Place a wooden Popsicle stick into each pop and freeze.

7. Peel off the paper cups when you're ready to eat your pops.

Haunted House Centerpieces

Hansel and Gretel couldn't resist the witch's candy house—and neither will your friends. These centerpieces are easy to make, and your guests will have sweet treats to take home.

What You Need:

* chocolate ready-to-spread frosting
* chocolate-flavored graham crackers
* Halloween candies (candy corn, gumdrops, peanut butter candies like Reese's Pieces, jellybeans)

* high-quality paper plates (the large and sturdy kind that have raised edges)
* serving spoon
* empty pint-size carton or container (from a dairy product) for each guest
* plastic knives

What You Do:

1. Have each guest turn her plate upside down to make a little "hill" for her haunted house to perch on.

2. Spoon a blob of chocolate frosting in the middle of each plate. Then, put the carton upside down on top of it and press down firmly. The frosting will harden and help keep the "house" in place while you work on it. Let it set for about 10 minutes.

3. Use more frosting as "mortar" to attach graham cracker "siding" to the house.

4. Use the serrated end of a plastic knife to cut the crackers to fit the peaks of the "roof."

5. When the house is covered in graham crackers, use more frosting to shingle the roof with candy corn, create gumdrop fences, and outline windows with peanut butter pieces and jellybeans. Go ahead and add any other decorative details that your sweet tooth desires.

Peanut Blossom Bug Eyes

What You Need:

* 1 bag (9 ounces) milk chocolate kisses
* 1/2 cup shortening
* 3/4 cup creamy or crunchy peanut butter
* 1/3 cup granulated sugar
* 1/3 cup packed light brown sugar
* 1 egg
* 2 tablespoons milk
* 1 teaspoon vanilla extract
* 1-1/2 cups all-purpose flour
* 1 teaspoon baking soda
* 1/2 teaspoon salt
* orange sugar crystals
* orange food coloring
* vanilla frosting
* chocolate sprinkles
* large bowl
* measuring cups and spoons
* mixing spoon
* medium bowl
* cookie sheet
* wire rack

What You Do:

1. Preheat the oven to 375°. Remove the wrappers from the milk chocolate kisses.

2. In a large bowl, beat shortening and peanut butter until well blended. Add the granulated sugar and the brown sugar; beat until light and fluffy. Add the egg, milk, and vanilla extract; beat well.

3. In a medium bowl, stir together flour, baking soda, and salt. Gradually, add the flour mixture to the peanut butter mixture. Stir until well blended.

4. Shape the dough into 1-inch balls.

5. Roll the dough balls in the orange sugar crystals. Place the balls onto an ungreased cookie sheet.

6. Bake for 10 to 12 minutes or until lightly browned.

7. Remove from the oven and immediately place a chocolate kiss on top of each cookie, pressing down so the cookie cracks around the circular edge.

8. Transfer to a wire rack. Let cool completely.

9. When cool, spread orange-tinted (from food-coloring) vanilla frosting around the edges of the cookie. Add three dots for eyes and a nose with plain white frosting. Press two chocolate sprinkles into the frosting eyes.

Spiderweb Peanut Butter Temptations

makes about 36

What You Need:

* 14-ounce package miniature peanut butter cups
* 1/2 cup (1 stick) butter or margarine, softened
* 1/2 cup packed light brown sugar
* 1/2 cup granulated sugar
* 1/2 cup creamy peanut butter
* 1 egg
* 1/2 teaspoon vanilla extract
* 1-1/2 cups all-purpose flour
* 3/4 teaspoon baking soda
* 1/2 teaspoon salt
* vanilla frosting
* measuirng cups and spoons
* muffin pans
* muffin liners
* large bowl
* wooden spoon
* medium bowl
* pastry bag or plastic sandwich bag with a corner snipped off

What You Do:

1. Preheat the oven to 375°. Remove wrappers from the peanut butter cup candies.

2. Line the muffin pans (1-3/4 inches in diameter) with paper muffin liners.

3. In a large bowl, beat the butter, brown sugar, granulated sugar, peanut butter, egg, and vanilla extract until light and fluffy.

4. In a medium bowl, stir together the flour, baking soda, and salt. Gradually, add the flour mixture to the peanut butter mixture in the large bowl, beating until well blended.

5. Shape dough into 1-inch balls. Place one ball in each prepared muffin cup. Don't flatten.

6. Bake for 10 to 12 minutes, until puffed and lightly browned.

7. Remove from the oven and immediately press a peanut butter cup on top of each treat. Let cool completely in the muffin pan.

8. When the treats are cool, draw a spiderweb on top with vanilla frosting, using a decorating tool like a pastry bag or plastic sandwich bag with a corner snipped off.

CREEPY CRAWLY CANDY CREATIONS

There's no cooking involved to make these spooky little candy sculptures, but assembly is required. Get ready to be bugged.

Mounds of Bugs

makes 24 bugs

What You Need:

* ❋ 24 snack-size Mounds candy bars
* ❋ 144 1-inch pieces pull-and-peel red licorice candy
* ❋ 1 cup prepared chocolate frosting
* ❋ 48 yellow candy-coated pieces (like M&M's or Reese's Pieces)

* ❋ sprinkles
* ❋ measuring cups
* ❋ skewers
* ❋ spoon
* ❋ pastry bag or plastic sandwich bag with a corner snipped off
* ❋ scissors

What You Do:

1. Using a skewer, poke three holes in each long side of the Mounds bars. Insert a piece of licorice in each hole to make legs.

2. Spoon frosting into either a pastry bag with a small plain tip or a small plastic sandwich bag with a corner snipped off. Pipe two small frosting dots on one short end of the candy bar, and attach yellow candy-coated pieces as eyes. Pipe icing dots on top of the eyes to make pupils. Add some other icing dots as spots on the bug bodies.

3. Press the sprinkles into the icing spots so each bug's body has multi-colored dots.

Spook-tacular Spiders

What You Need:

* 24 Peppermint Patties
* 24 rectangular butter cookies (store-bought)
* 1 cup vanilla frosting
* blue and red sprinkles
* measuring cups

* butter knife (for spreading)
* pastry bag or plastic sandwich bag with a corner snipped off
* scissors
* spoon

What You Do:

1. Attach the Peppermint Patties to the butter cookies by spreading a small amount of frosting as the "glue."

2. Spoon frosting into either a pastry bag with a small plain tip or a small plastic sandwich bag with a corner snipped off. Pipe eight legs, two eyes, and a nose on the patties.

3. Press two blue sprinkles into the frosting dots for the eyes and one red sprinkle for the nose.

Creepy Critters

makes 24 critters

What You Need:

* orange food coloring
* 1 cup vanilla frosting
* 24 milk chocolate nuggets
* 24 rectangular butter cookies (store-bought)
* 1/2 cup chocolate frosting
* 48 orange-coated candies (or Reese's Pieces)

* 24 chocolate sprinkles
* measuring cups
* small bowl
* mixing spoon
* butter knife (for spreading)
* pastry bag or plastic sandwich bag with a corner snipped off
* scissors

What You Do:

1. In a small bowl, add a few drops of orange food coloring to the vanilla frosting, and mix well.

2. Attach the nuggets to the butter cookies by spreading a small amount of the orange frosting as "glue."

3. Spoon the chocolate frosting into either a pastry bag with a small plain tip or a small plastic sandwich bag with a corner snipped off. Pipe eight legs onto each cookie and two eyes and a nose onto each nugget.

4. Press two coated candies into the frosting for eyes and a sprinkle into the frosting for the nose.

MEGA NEW YEAR'S EVE BASH

Make a grand entrance into the New Year with style and panache. You know—a formal affair. Invite your closest friends to a most debonair party.

INVITES

Hats off to this great invitation idea!

What You Need:

* black construction paper
* pencil
* scissors
* metallic paint-pens
* black envelopes
* silver or gold pens

What You Do:

1. Fold a piece of black construction paper in half the short way. Using a pencil, draw an image of a top hat with the top of the hat being on the fold. Cut it out carefully with a pair of scissors (just be sure to leave the fold intact).

2. On the fronts of the cards, write the following message using metallic paint-pens: "You are cordially invited to a gala night. Can't top that!"

3. On the inside, write all the party info. Be sure to tell your guests it's a formal affair and that they should show up in glamour wear. That means sequined dresses, black velvet gowns with pearls, cocktail dresses, tuxes (they can dig out some old "dress-up" clothes or find this kind of stuff in a secondhand clothing store for cheap).

4. Mail the invites in black envelopes addressed using silver or gold ink.

DÉCOR

For that oh-so-chic atmosphere, be sure to have plenty of black and white helium balloons with silver and gold string all over your party room. Place several bowls of confetti around the room—and enough party hats and noise-makers for everyone. Frame all the doors and windows with tiny white holiday lights.

Make party poppers by covering empty toilet paper tubes with aluminum foil or elegant-looking wrapping paper, leaving plenty of excess paper on the ends. Secure wrapping with tape in the middle, gently twist one end, and tie a fancy ribbon around it. Pour jellybeans into the open end before twisting and tying it closed, too.

For the right musical ambience, make a rockin' track of last year's big— or at least big-for-a-week—hits. If you don't feel like making your own tape, twirl the radio dial until you find a countdown special. This should be as easy as finding rides at an amusement park.

TO DO

Top It Off: As soon as guests arrive, top things off by making party hats. Poster board works best because it's stiff. Bend it around to make a simple conical hat shape, and staple it in place. Then add all kinds of stuff, like glitter, feathers, beads, paint, markers, streamers, anything. Use whatever you think would make a primo party hat. You just can't usher in the New Year without one!

Signing Up: One of the best ways to welcome the New Year is to bid farewell to the old one with a "Remember the Good Old Days" mural. First, place a large piece of white poster board on the floor, and lay out tons of markers, colored pencils, crayons, and other doodling tools. Have all your buds gather around to create an image that's "totally last year." Maybe it's a drawing of a beautiful park you guys visited last year, or some inside jokes that you made up, or some really embarrassing moment you all shared. If you're truly artistic, make a little comic strip of the whole gang hangin' out together. If drawing is not your thing, write down some sentimental song lyrics you all enjoyed listening to together. Your images can be sweet, sentimental, or downright hilarious. When you're finished, hang the mural on a wall as a "Happy New Year" banner.

"I Predict...": Ask everyone to write New Year predictions on notebook paper, and to include a list of all the styles, foods, songs, and other trends they think will be huge in the coming year. You can also make personal predictions ("I predict Megan will finally admit that she has a big crush on Jason!"). Then read aloud your guesses to each other, sign them, and place them in a shoe box. Put the box in a safe spot you'll easily be able to locate next year. Think of how hilarious it will be to read the predictions at the next big bash 365 days later!

Gotta Pop a Piñata: Fill a piñata (see page 60) with noisemakers, streamers, confetti, and lots of candy. Blindfold one guest at a time with a scarf, spin her around five times, and let her take three swings. It's good for lots of laughs, because you can get pretty dizzy!

The Confetti: Before the party, use a funnel to put confetti inside some balloons before blowing them up. Then, at the party, give each girl a balloon and a safety pin. Throw the balloons in the air and pop them with the pins. (Be careful not to stick a friend by mistake.) The confetti flies all over the place. Don't forget to break out those noise-makers!

EATS

You'll be starting this party way after dinnertime, so you don't need to worry about a big meal, but that doesn't let you off the culinary hook. Set out plenty of nibbles, like cheese and crackers, plates of veggies and dip, and snacks, like pretzels, chips, and cookies. That way, your friends will have plenty to munch on throughout the night. When the clock gets close to midnight, break out the festive glasses and sparkling punch. Get ready to toast!

Sparkling Punch

serves 16

What You Need:

* 2-liter bottle lemon-lime soda
* 2-liter bottle lemon-lime seltzer water
* 12-ounce can frozen juice concentrate in a berry blend favor
* limes wedges to garnish each glass
* punch bowl
* mixing spoon
* ice

What You Do:

1. To make the punch, pour the soda, seltzer, and the juice concentrate into the punch bowl. Stir until the concentrate has dissolved.

2. Carefully place some ice in the punch bowl and serve with lime wedges for garnish.

A VALENTINE NIGHT SPA FOR THE GIRLS

Who better to spend Valentine's Day with than the ones you love most— your BFF's! Invite all your gal pals to spend V Day night hanging out, chowing, and beautifying. This can be a sleepover, or just a great night of chilling.

INVITES

Get some cream-colored note cards and matching envelopes, and stamp them with heart-shaped rubber stamps dipped in pink and red ink. Let them dry overnight. Once dry, use a fine-point black pen to add party details.

Now, for the fun part—getting your friends involved. Assign each guest a different set of duties. Think about each girl, and then assign her one of the roles below. Punch a hole in each invite and, with ribbon, attach a pink piece of paper with instructions for what each girl should bring to the party....

1. Spa Goddess

Who takes indulgent, rose-scented bubble baths? Who stocks up on lavish lotions and moisturizing masks? Your Spa Goddess, of course, and she's in charge of whipping up masks before the party (tell her to keep the masks refrigerated until ready to use). Here are some recipes for homemade masks that will leave your guests looking gorgeous (both recipes make enough for 2 masks).

Oatmeal mask for regular-to-oily skin
Ingredients: 1 cup cooked oatmeal (don't use instant, and let it cool first!), 1 teaspoon honey, 1 teaspoon wheat germ

Avocado mask for regular-to-dry skin
Ingredients: 1 very ripe avocado (mashed), 1 teaspoon lemon juice, 1 teaspoon mayonnaise

What You Do:

1. Mix the ingredients together in a bowl, and slather on your face (avoiding the areas around your eyes).

2. Let the mask sit for 10 minutes, then rinse it off with warm water.

2. Manicure Magician

Which of your buds has glitter polish in tons of shades? Your Manicure Magician should bring all the nail goodies. Her list should include nail files, cotton balls, polish remover, cuticle pushers, clippers, and hand cream for everyone. Since she already has a collection of manicure necessities, it shouldn't cost a bundle (and other buds can pitch in).

3. Makeup Maven

Which of your gal pals spends her Saturday afternoons looking for fun new cosmetics? Is she the proud owner of 11 shades of gloss and 12 lip brushes? She's your Makeup Maven. Ask her to bring her makeup kit so she can give makeovers to all the guests! She should be packin' cleanser, eye glitter, blush, application sponges, and whatever else she can fit in her cosmetics case!

4. Hollywood Hotshot

Who's first in line for every movie opening? Who can quote *Austin Powers* without missing a beat? This pal is your Hollywood Hotshot, for, after all, what's a slumber party without a bunch of chick flicks? Here are a few Valentine's Day vid suggestions. Your hotshot might already have these titles in her alphabetized collection (A couple packs of microwave popcorn, Twizzlers, and Milk Duds can complete her list!):

* *Beauty and the Beast*
* *Ever After*
* *Father of the Bride*
* *My Best Friend's Wedding*
* *The Princess Bride*
* *Sabrina*
* *Sixteen Candles*
* *Titanic*

5. Mix Master

Does she know the words to every song on the Top 10? Have your Mix Master bring her rockin' CD collection, portable CD player, and (if she has one) a karaoke machine to the party. She's also the one to organize your lip-synching contest.

6. Cuisine Queens

Even if they don't know their way around the kitchen, get the rest of your guests—Cuisine Queens—busy with food prep. Read on for some super delicious recipes that your guests can help you with.

DÉCOR

Figure out where you and your crew can hang. Is your room big enough? Is the basement cozy enough to sleep in? (Be sure to banish the dust bunnies.) Once you've picked your place, get decorating! Fill the room with pretty frilly pillows and warm, cozy blankets. Add some potpourri and simple vases of fresh flowers to tabletops. You can also sprinkle real rose petals around the room for a girly touch.

The day of the party, set the table with floral paper plates, cups, and napkins. Then add matching pink plastic utensils (make sure you have enough for dinner, dessert, and breakfast, if it's a sleepover). If mom has a pretty linen tablecloth, ask if you can use it. Put out fresh flowers and scented candles as centerpieces.

TO DO

Organize your evening so it best suits you and your friends. Spa Goddess should get out the goop and slather the masks on your guests.

Next, get your Manicure Magician to pick out the perfect polishes for dynamite digits. Then it's makeover time. One of your Cuisine Queens might want to check out how she looks in green glitter eye shadow!

Don't forget to turn on the tunes! Have your Mix Master lead everyone in a karaoke/lip-synching contest. For an encore, every girl can perform a mushy love song plucked from a hat.

EATS

All dishes featured here are for the night of the party. Assuming you didn't keep the 'rents up till sunrise, ask your folks to help with the scrambled eggs, bagels, and OJ the next morning (if it's a sleepover).

Cranberry Spritzers
serves 12

What You Need:

* ice cubes
* 64-ounce jug cranberry juice
* 2-liter bottle club soda
* lime
* drinking glasses

What You Do:

1. Place ice cubes in glasses.
2. Fill each glass three-quarters full of cranberry juice, then top each glass with club soda.
3. Finish with a squeeze of lime, and serve.

Chili Cheese Dip

serves 6—make ahead

What You Need:

* 2 8-ounce tubs soft cream cheese
* 1 cup mayonnaise
* 8 ounces shredded cheddar or Monterey Jack cheese
* 1/2 cup mild salsa
* 1 tomato, chopped (optional)
* 3 scallions, chopped (optional)
* tortilla chips
* measuring cups
* glass casserole dish
* mixing spoon
* spatula
* plastic wrap

What You Do:

1. Place the cream cheese in a shallow glass casserole dish. Add mayonnaise, shredded cheese, and salsa. Mix well, then smooth over the top evenly with a spatula. Cover with plastic wrap and refrigerate.

2. At the party, heat the dip in the microwave on high for about 4 minutes or until heated through—or you can heat the dip in the oven for 20 minutes at 350°.

3. Sprinkle the top with chopped tomato and chopped scallion, if desired. Serve hot with tortilla chips.

Baked Ziti Casserole

serves 10-12—make ahead

What You Need:

* 1 medium onion, chopped
* 3 garlic cloves, minced
* 3 tablespoons olive oil
* 28-ounce can tomato puree
* 1 teaspoon dried oregano
* 1 teaspoon dried basil
* 1/2 teaspoon dried red pepper flakes
* salt and pepper to taste
* 1 pound (16 ounces) dried ziti pasta
* 2 large eggs
* 1 cup half-and-half
* 4 cups shredded mozzarella
* 1/4 cup grated Parmesan
* measuring cups and spoons
* large saucepan
* metal spatula
* large pot
* colander
* large casserole dish
* whisk
* plastic wrap

What You Do:

1. In a large saucepan over medium heat, cook the onion and garlic in olive oil until softened.

2. Add the tomato puree, oregano, basil, red pepper flakes, and salt and pepper to taste. Simmer the mixture for about 5 minutes, stirring with a metal spatula until well combined and slightly thickened.

3. Meanwhile, in a large pot, cook the pasta according to the package directions, then drain in a colander.

4. In the bottom of a large casserole dish, whisk together the eggs and half-and-half. Add the drained hot ziti and toss to coat.

5. Add 3 cups of the mozzarella, stirring well. Spread the tomato mixture evenly in the dish, and top with the remaining 1 cup mozzarella and the Parmesan. Cover with plastic wrap, and let it cool. Store in the refrigerator.

6. At the party, preheat the oven to 350°. Remove the plastic wrap and bake the ziti for approximately 40 minutes or until bubbly and golden brown. Serve hot.

Garlic Bread

serves 10-12—make ahead

What You Need:

* several loaves of French or Italian bread (cut open lengthwise)
* 1/2 cup (1 stick) butter, melted
* 1 egg
* 1/4 cup grated Parmesan cheese
* 1 teaspoon garlic salt
* measuring cups and spoons
* bread knife
* mixing bowl
* mixing spoon
* aluminum foil

What You Do:

1. Open the top of the loaves, lengthwise. Set aside.

2. In a mixing bowl, combine the melted butter and egg. Add the cheese and garlic salt, stirring well. Brush, pour, or spoon this sauce down the length of the split of each loaf of bread. Then, wrap loaves individually, in aluminum foil.

3. At the party, preheat the oven to 350°. Place foil-wrapped bread in oven for 20 minutes or until warm. Place on a serving platter or cutting board, cut into thick slices and serve.

Double Chocolate Brownie Sundaes

serves 9—make brownies ahead, assemble sundaes at party

What You Need:

* 12 ounce package semi-sweet chocolate morsels
* 1/2 cup (1 stick) butter, cut into pieces
* 3 large eggs
* 1/4 cup flour
* 1 cup sugar
* 1 teaspoon vanilla extract
* 1/4 teaspoon baking soda
* 1 gallon vanilla ice cream
* warm Peanut Butter Cup Sauce (see recipe to follow)

* whipped cream
* chopped nuts
* maraschino cherries for garnish
* 8 x 8-inch baking pan
* heavy saucepan
* measuring cups and spoons
* whisk
* spatula
* aluminum foil or plastic wrap
* serving dishes
* ice cream scoop

What You Do:

1. Preheat the oven to 350°. Grease an 8 x 8-inch baking pan.

2. In a heavy saucepan over medium heat, melt 8 ounces of chocolate morsels and butter, stirring until smooth. Remove pan from the heat, and stir in the eggs, using the whisk to combine.

3. Add the flour, sugar, vanilla extract, and baking soda, and whisk until smooth. With a spatula, stir in the remaining chocolate morsels.

4. Scrape the mixture into a pan and smooth over the top. Bake for about 25 minutes or until brownies pull away from the sides of the pan. Remove from the oven, and let it cool completely.

5. Cover the pan tightly with aluminum foil or plastic wrap. At the party, cut the brownies into squares and place in serving dishes. Top each brownie with a scoop of vanilla ice cream, Warm Peanut Butter Cup Sauce (see following recipe), whipped cream, chopped nuts, and a cherry.

Warm Peanut Butter Cup Sauce

make ahead

What You Need:

* 2 tablespoons butter
* 2 tablespoons firmly packed brown sugar
* 2 tablespoons light corn syrup
* 1/3 cup creamy peanut butter
* 1 cup half-and-half
* 8 ounces milk chocolate chips
* 1 tablespoon vanilla extract
* nuts (optional)
* measuring cups and spoons
* heavy saucepan
* whisk
* plastic container with lid
* small saucepan

What You Do:

1. In a heavy saucepan over medium heat, melt the butter, brown sugar, and corn syrup. Using a whisk, mix in the peanut butter and half-and-half, and whisk until smooth.

2. Bring the mixture to a slow simmer. Add the chocolate chips, and whisk until completely melted and smooth. Add the vanilla extract, stirring to combine. Transfer the mixture to a plastic container with a lid and store in the refrigerator.

3. When ready to serve, spoon the sauce into a small saucepan and heat on low until warmed through. Drip the sauce over the ice cream. Top with nuts and stuff.

PARTY GRAS

What? You've never heard of Mardi Gras? It's one of the best party holidays ever! In New Orleans, the most famous home of Mardi Gras, there are two weeks (always held the two weeks leading up to Ash Wednesday) of music, costume balls, and parades, as well as beads galore! But you don't have to live in Louisiana to celebrate, and you can hold a Mardi Gras costume party anytime.

INVITES

Y'all come! Mask-shaped invitations are stylin'—plus they remind guests to dress in costume. First, fold a piece of construction paper in half the short way. Draw a mask shape, and making sure not to cut the fold, cut it out. Since your mask is on one side of the fold, it opens like a card. Write party details on the inside, including the costume party theme. Decorate the invite in Mardi Gras colors—purple (which stands for justice), green (faith), and gold (power). Feathers, sequins, and ribbons make great accents.

DÉCOR

Carry the Mardi Gras color scheme into your party décor with foil ribbon and streamers. Or make like a New Orleans resident and drape fabric or colored ribbon from your front porch or balcony. A banner with a favorite Mardi Gras saying in French, like "Laissez les bons temps rouler!" (translation: "Let the good times roll!"), makes a festive impression. To incorporate a Mardi Gras tradition, yank some beads out of storage and hang them on door frames, tables, your dog—anything. Use construction paper to make masks for hanging.

Conjure up the mood by jazzing your party with New Orleans faves Harry Connick Jr., Branford Marsalis, Dr. John, or Louis Armstrong. Feeling adventurous? Try zydeco music. Instead of spending cash on CD's, check the library—if they have disks, just use your library card!

TO DO

Join the Krewe: Turn party patrons into a Mardi Gras *krewe* (say "crew")—a group of people who organize a parade or costume ball. But your krewe can just have a ball...period. First, choose a funky name. Some famous krewe names are Orpheus and Rex, but make up your own. To get your krewe into the spirit, hold a costume contest. Unlike scary Halloween costumes, Mardi Gras costumes are colorful and fun, so give awards for the silliest, most elaborate, and most creative.

You can also get your krewe to make throws—prizes traditionally tossed from Mardi Gras parade floats or New Orleans balconies. The most famous throws are beads, but plastic cups, Frisbees, and *doubloons* (decorative aluminum coins) are popular, too. Your throws will make great *lagniappe* (that's French for "an extra unexpected gift") for guests to take home!

Free Throw: Since throws are a big part of Mardi Gras, practice your aim! Here's how to play:

> ✳ Divide your krewe into groups of two, and give each pair a Frisbee and a 33-inch-long string of beads.

> ✳ One person holds the string of beads with both hands to their side (don't hold the beads right in front of you or you might get hit in the face!), so that it makes a circle or oval.

> ✳ The other person stands five feet away and tries to throw the Frisbee through the beads.

> ✳ Each time the Frisbee makes it through, the two teammates should each take a step back—and no giant steps allowed!

> ✳ The pair ending up the farthest apart wins. This game can also be played with a plastic cup and beads—try to toss the beads into the cup.

EATS

You'll be happy to learn that real New Orleans cuisine is awesome! Spicy faves include red beans and rice, jambalaya (a spicy rice and seafood dish), gumbo (a thick seafood stew), and po' boys (huge sandwiches like the one in the following recipe). To become a gourmet the easy way, try ready-made red beans and rice mixes (check the rice section of your grocery store). Cook according to package directions, and voilà!

Mardi Gras Po' Boys

What You Need:

* 8 6-inch hoagie rolls
* various condiments—
  mayonnaise, mustard, Italian
  salad dressing, ranch dressing
* 1/2 pound of sliced cheese
  (American, swiss or mozzarella—
  or any other kind you like)

* deli coldcuts, like turkey, ham,
  or roastbeef, 1/2 pound of each
  (optional)
* 1/2 head of iceberg lettuce
* 2 ripe tomatoes, thinly sliced
* sliced pickles
* butter knife

What You Do:

1. Open each hoagie roll, lengthwise.

2. Using a butter knife, spread a layer of your selected condiments on the top half of each hoagie roll.

3. Pile on a couple of slices of cheese and meat on each hoagie roll half, alternating the meat and cheese, if you are having both.

4. Top the cheese (and meat) with 2 to 3 pieces of lettuce and tomato. Finish off your po' with any additional toppings, like pickles.

Chapter 7

Terrific Theme Festivities

Birthdays and holidays are a natural for parties. But why not make a party feel extra special by giving your gathering a theme? Themes make parties extra fun—and they're great anytime of year! Plus, you can plan every aspect of your party around that theme—invites, food, décor, and more. And all this time you thought "theme" was just that stuff your English teacher talks about when she assigns book reports!

TEA PARTY

If you think tea parties are for dolls and teddy bears, think again! They're an excellent excuse for you and your friends to get together on a lovely weekend afternoon. If the weather is nice and sunny, you can have your tea party outside in the backyard or on a sun porch. Just be sure to ask your folks before breaking out that fine china. (Oh, did we say *breaking*?) Hey, your everyday dishes can be just as fine!

INVITES

What You Need:

* good-quality, fancy cream-colored paper
* a calligraphy pen
* tea bags

What You Do:

1. Because a tea party is supposed to seem somewhat uppity, give your invitations a fancy flair. Use a good-quality, cream-colored paper to make cards, and write the party info with a calligraphy pen. Ask your guests to dress in their tea-party best (you know—like something lacy that you haven't worn since your aunt's wedding).

2. For a fun touch, tuck a tea bag into each envelope before sealing.

DÉCOR

The most important part of decorating for a tea party is the table setting. A tea party calls for real chairs—not crashing out on the floor or flopping in beanbags—so have enough seating available. Be sure to get a pretty lace or floral tablecloth to cover the serving table. A beautiful centerpiece adds a nice touch; fresh flowers arranged in a decorative teapot, for example. Before your guests arrive, set the table with dishes, flatware, and napkins.

TO DO

Be Mad Hatters!: A few days before the party, gather up some supplies for you and your friends to make funky straw hats. Get plain straw hats from the craft or discount store (or see if you and your buds can gather old ones from around your houses). The day of the party, set out the hats, a few bottles of tacky glue, and a whole bunch of hat decorations—silk and dried flowers, beads, buttons, ribbon, old scarves, pieces of junk jewelry, whatever. So the hats will have time to dry, make them as soon as your guests arrive. That way, you can wear your funny hats while having tea! Afterwards, your friends can take their hats home and hang them on their bedroom walls. (No wearing these out in public after the party, OK?)

EATS

The hit of any tea party is a delicious menu of yummy, easy-to-make goodies. Tea sandwiches are assembled, cut out with cute-shaped cookie cutters, and served up on a pretty platter covered with doilies. With a little help from your favorite grown-up, make these delicious sandwiches the morning of the party and keep them refrigerated before serving. If you make them the night before, the mayo could spoil and the bread might stiffen...ew!

Tuna Salad Tea Sandwiches

serves 4

What You Need:

* 2 celery stalks
* 1 apple
* 1 can albacore tuna in water
* 1/4 cup mayonnaise
* salt and pepper to taste
* 8 slices wheat bread, crusts removed
* measuring cups
* knife
* large bowl
* cookie cutters

What You Do:

1. Chop the celery and apple into small pieces. Then, combine all the ingredients (except the bread) in a large bowl.

2. Spread the mixture onto the bread, and cut out the sandwiches with cookie cutters.

Egg Salad Tea Sandwiches

serves 4

What You Need:

* 3 eggs
* 1/4 cup mayonnaise
* 1 tablespoon Dijon mustard
* salt and pepper, to taste
* 1 teaspoon dried dill
* 8 slices white bread, crusts removed

* measuring cups and spoons
* saucepan
* spoon
* sharp knife
* bowl
* cookie cutters

What You Do:

1. Boil the eggs (approximately 10 to 15 minutes) in a saucepan. When cool, peel the eggs and chop them. Combine the chopped eggs with the rest of the ingredients (except the bread) in the bowl.

2. Spread the mixture onto the bread, and cut out the sandwiches with cookie cutters.

Cucumber Tea Sandwiches

serves 4

What You Need:

* 1 cucumber, chopped
* 4 ounces softened cream cheese (plain)
* 1 teaspoon lemon juice
* salt and pepper, to taste
* 8 slices of white bread, crusts removed

* measuring spoons
* bowl
* spoon
* cookie cutters

What You Do:

1. Combine all of the ingredients (except the bread) in a bowl. Mix well.

2. Spread the mixture onto the bread, and cut out the sandwiches with cookie cutters.

Mini Confetti Tea Cakes

serves 8

What You Need:

* vanilla cake mix (and all the ingredients required according to the box directions)
* food coloring
* 3 cups of whipped cream topping
* rainbow sprinkles
* medium bowl
* wooden spoon (to mix the batter)
* measuring cups
* muffin pan (that holds 12 cups)
* cupcake liners
* toothpicks
* butter knife

What You Do:

1. Make and bake the cupcakes following the box directions, lining each muffin cup with a cupcake liner.

2. Remove cupcakes from the oven and let them cool completely. When cool, remove them from the muffin pan, but keeping the liners on.

3. Using a toothpick, poke holes (as many as you want) in the top of each cupcake.

4. Then, carefully squeeze a few drops of food coloring (any or as many colors as you like) into each poked hole. The color will soak into the cake, so when you eat it, it's an artistic surprise.

5. Using a butter knife, spread a thin layer of whipped cream topping over the top of each cupcake. Add some rainbow sprinkles to the top for the finished confetti look.

FALL FEST

Colored leaves blanket your backyard, and there's a crispness to the air. Why not cook up some festive fall food and party down country-style?

INVITES

Make your pals personal paper pumpkin invites. Just fold orange construction paper horizontally and cut out a wide half circle (the way you do when you make heart valentines). Unfold the paper, and voilà—a pumpkin! Well, sort of. With a little glue, attach a green paper stem. Pen in your party details. With a black pen, draw arcs from the stem of your pumpkin down to the bottom. Be careful not to draw lines over your party info—just stop and restart your arcs in those spots.

Once your invites are complete, drop them in envelopes, decorated with festive fall stickers or cutouts. Pop them in the mail, and wait for the phone to ring. In the meantime, get planning.

DÉCOR

Convert your back porch, garage, or basement into a country barn. We know—it's a stretch, but a little imagination, a plethora of pumpkins, and a few scattered scarecrows can work wonders! Wherever you choose to throw your harvest fest, be sure it's a large, open area. You'll also need a long table for a buffet, or a couple of card tables. If you have picnic tables, haul 'em into your barn.

Very large pumpkins and bales of hay (try your local produce stand) make great seats! Other than that, creating your fall festival is totally up to you. You can find just about everything you need to create a fall utopia (hey, rhymes with cornucopia!) at any craft store or at a local farm stand. Look for scarecrows, corn husks, gourds, baskets, hay bales, and garlands of colorful leaves. Brainstorm. Whatever feels like autumn works.

Cover a buffet table with an old patchwork quilt, a checkered tablecloth, or even canvas potato sacks. (Cut open the sacks and lay them flat.) Decorate your buffet table with all your gathered goodies.

Do your folks save every little thing? If so, head to the basement or attic and look for old baskets, serving trays, weathered vases, anything country-ish. Wrap the rims and handles of baskets with garlands of fall leaves, and fill them with mini pumpkins, squash and gourds, along with autumn fruits like apples, grapes, pomegranates, and cranberries.

Wrap cutlery in colorful bandanas, and place them in an earthy-looking crock. Guests can then use the bandanas as napkins. Set out enough plates and cups for your guests. Use one-of-a-kind old plates from a yard sale or junk shop, or take the simple route and use colorful paper plates and cups. Don't forget to spin some country tunes. Dixie Chicks, anyone?

TO DO

Create-a-Crow

Turn on the tunes and make scarecrows. Ask guests to bring infant one-piece sleepers (the kind with feet attached) to your get-together so they can make their own baby scarecrows! As the Fall Fest hostess, you supply the rest of the materials—they're all inexpensive. These baby scarecrows make adorable fall decorations.

What You Need:

* pantyhose
* plastic grocery bags
* infant sleepers
* safety pins
* markers
* buttons
* felt pieces
* straw
* yarn
* scissors
* child-size hat
* ribbon bows

What You Do:

1. Knot each leg of the pantyhose.

2. Stuff the middle section or waist of the pantyhose with plastic grocery bags. This will be the head. Knot it closed.

3. Stuff the infant sleeper with lots of plastic bags in the legs, arms, and body.

4. Secure the pantyhose head onto the neck of the sleeper using safety pins. Hide the pantyhose legs in the sleeper.

5. Decorate the pantyhose face with markers, buttons, and felt pieces. Stuff straw into the arm openings and around the neck.

6. Use yarn for hair. Attach a child-size hat or ribbon bows to the head.

Pumpkin Face Contest

Have a pumpkin-decorating contest! Tell your guests there will be anonymous voting for the scariest, funniest, ugliest, most realistic, or whatever category of pumpkin faces you choose. The easiest way to decorate your pumpkins is to paint them. You'll need pumpkins in various sizes (at least one for each guest), and plenty of paintbrushes and acrylic craft paints in every color of the rainbow. If you want, put out some glue, glitter, googly eyes, buttons, feathers, and other stuff for your pumpkin faces. Don't forget to lay down some newspaper to avoid messes, and to put out cups of water for cleaning brushes.

Line up the finished pumpkin masterpieces, and assign each one a number. Give every guest a piece of paper and a pencil. Decide which category you're voting for first and have everyone drop their votes into a (straw) hat. Tally up the votes, and make sure your winner gets a Fall Fest blue ribbon (and a cool prize)!

EATS

Make sure you have some snacks and fresh apple cider for your guests. Scatter small pumpkin-shaped bowls or those plastic trick-or-treating jack-o'-lanterns on the buffet table, and fill 'em with tortilla chips, pretzels, or trail mix. Make a pleasing plate of purple grapes and alternating green and red apple slices. Pair the fresh fruit with a bowl of peanut butter, warm caramel, or Fruity Fall Dip (recipe follows) for dunking—don't forget toothpicks and festive napkins!

Halfway through the party—after your guests have worked up an appetite—bring out the main meal. Keep your menu harvest-related with fall ingredients like cranberries, pumpkins, apples, corn, and potatoes. If you have some delish family recipes, go ahead and use them. If not, we have some simple recipes for your harvest feast.

Fruity Fall Dip

makes 3 cups

What You Need:

* 8 ounces softened cream cheese
* 8 ounces vanilla yogurt
* 5 tablespoons honey
* 1 teaspoon cinnamon
* 1/2 teaspoon nutmeg
* measuring spoons
* mixing bowl
* spoon
* serving bowl
* plastic wrap

What You Do:

1. In a bowl, beat the cream cheese until it's smooth and creamy. Add the rest of the ingredients and mix well.

2. Spoon into a serving bowl, cover with plastic wrap, and refrigerate for at least three hours. Stir before serving.

Turkey Sandwich Roll-ups

makes 4

What You Need:

- ✳ 4 10-inch whole-wheat tortillas
- ✳ 1/2 ripe California avocado
- ✳ 1/2 pound roast turkey, thinly sliced
- ✳ 1/2 pound of your favorite cheese slices, like Swiss, muenster, or cheddar
- ✳ 2 tomatoes, thinly sliced
- ✳ shredded lettuce
- ✳ 1 cucumber, sliced
- ✳ small bowl
- ✳ fork (for mashing)
- ✳ butter knife
- ✳ toothpicks
- ✳ mayonnaise
- ✳ honey mustard

What You Do:

1. Lay each tortilla flat. Peel the avocado and mash it to a pulp in a small bowl. Spread the avocado evenly on each tortilla. Arrange the turkey slices on top of the avocado, on one half of the open tortillas.

2. Top the turkey slices with cheese, tomatoes, lettuce, and cucumber slices. Roll up each tortilla tightly, leaving the ends open.

3. Halve each tortilla diagonally with a knife and keep the roll-ups secure with toothpicks. Serve with mayonnaise and honey mustard on the side.

Veggie Mashed Potatoes

Serves 4

What You Need:

- ✳ 1 20-ounce package frozen mashed potatoes
- ✳ 4 large carrots, peeled and sliced into 1/2-inch slices
- ✳ 3 parsnips, peeled and chopped into 1-inch cubes
- ✳ 4 stalks celery chopped
- ✳ 1/3 cup heavy cream
- ✳ 6 tablespoons butter
- ✳ pinch of nutmeg
- ✳ salt and pepper, to taste
- ✳ measuring cups and spoons
- ✳ large pot
- ✳ large bowl
- ✳ fork

What You Do:

1. Prepare potatoes according to package directions.

2. Put vegetables in a large pot, and cover with water. Bring to a boil. Simmer for 20 to 25 minutes or until vegetables are very tender. Drain.

3. Return veggies to a pot, or place in a large bowl. Stir in the heavy cream, butter, nutmeg, salt, and pepper. Then, mash vegetable mixture with a fork until smooth.

4. Mix into prepared mashed potatoes. Serve it hot.

Perfect Pumpkin Cheesecake

serves 12

What You Need:

* 2 cups graham cracker crumbs
* 8 tablespoons melted butter
* 24 ounces softened cream cheese
* 1 cup sugar
* 3/4 cup brown sugar
* 5 eggs
* 2 teaspoons pumpkin pie spice
* 1/4 cup heavy cream

* 16 ounces canned pumpkin
* measuring cups and spoons
* 9-inch springform pan
* electric mixer
* large bowl
* medium bowl
* wire rack
* an adult to help

Topping:

* mix together 6 tablespoons butter, softened, with 1 cup of brown sugar

* 1 cup of pecans or walnuts, chopped

What You Do:

1. Preheat oven to 325°.

2. Blend the graham cracker crumbs and 8 tablespoons of melted butter in a large bowl.

3. Press the mixture firmly over the bottom and up the sides of a lightly buttered 9-inch springform pan. Chill in the refrigerator.

4. Ask an adult to help using an electric mixer, and beat the cream cheese until very smooth in a medium bowl.

5. Add the sugar and brown sugar. Beat until well mixed.

6. Mix in the eggs one at a time until light and fluffy.

7. Beat in the pumpkin spice and heavy cream at low speed.

8. Mix in the canned pumpkin. Pour the mixture into the springform pan's chilled graham cracker crust.

9. Bake for 1 hour 35 minutes. Remove from the oven.

10. Spread the butter/brown sugar topping on the still-warm cheesecake and sprinkle with the nuts.

11. Put back into the oven for 10 minutes. Remove, and let it cool on a wire rack. Refrigerate overnight.

FUN-DO FEST

Love to play with your food? Love to get together and have fun with your friends? Well then you are going to love fondue! You may have heard of dishes like chocolate or cheese fondue.

It's so fun because you and your friends gather around a fondue pot (it's like a saucepan with a little flame underneath it) and dip your fave foods into melted chocolate or cheese. If you don't have a fondue set, you can make everything in a regular saucepan and when it's time to eat, gather around the stove and carefully dip your munchies into the sauce.

When the chocolate or cheese is melted, everyone grabs a special fondue fork (it's superlong, with two tiny spokes), spears a chunk of bread (for cheese), or something yummy like cake or fruit (for chocolate). Since you all share the same pot, it's a great way to have fun with your friends and play with your food!

So ask your folks to dig out that old-school fondue pot they've had since before you were born, then read on for the fondue-mentals....

INVITES

Fondue is perfect for small cozy gatherings, but the whole cooking-together thing also makes a fondue fiesta ideal for introducing a new bud or two to your crew. There's something about commiserating over losing every other marshmallow in a pot of chocolate that just makes for instant friendships!

After you've made a list of your grooviest pals, fold pieces of neutral-colored, heavy-stock paper, and write the party details inside. Then, using colored construction paper, make cutout images of fondue pots, triangles of Swiss cheese, or pieces of fruit. Glue them onto your invites and voilà!

PARTY PREP

Gather up your fondue pots. Ideally, you'll have one fondue pot for every four people, so if you're having a party of eight, you'll want at least two pots. If it's possible to borrow a couple of extra pots, that'd be great. If you have a different pot for every dish, you can minimize the time between courses, because you won't have to wash your pot after every different type of fondue.

Fondue sets often come with six to eight fondue forks. Each guest should have one fork to use for each course. Also, be sure to have some decorative serving platters—like one for the bread (for dipping in the cheese), and one for the fruit (for dipping in the chocolate).

And what's a fondue party without a little retro ambience? Because fondue is a throwback to the '70s, go for beanbag chairs, lava lamps, and shaggy throw rugs to set the scene.

TO DO

Go for retro activities like Twister and Charades. Or try something new. Even though fishing for tidbits of food in the fondue pot is the main activity at this party, why not go fishing as a fun party activity, too?

Fishing for Prizes: Hit the dollar store before the party to stock up on fun, cheap prizes (think of the stuff you find in a metal grabbing claw machine at the arcade). Then, cut out a whole bunch of colorful construction paper fish shapes, and write the name of a prize on both sides of each cutout. Attach one paper clip to each fish, and spread the shapes out in the center of the party area. Don't spread them too far apart, but make sure they aren't overlapping, either. Guests can take turns "fishing" for prizes using a rod you create—by tying a piece of string to the end of a long stick and tying a magnet to the other end of the string. Be sure to put the prizes out in plain view so guests know which goodies they want to go fish for.

EATS

Buy a few nice loaves of French or Italian bread from the bakery to tear into pieces for dipping into the cheese fondue. Bread and veggies are the best for the cheese fondue. Store-bought pound cake, brownies, angel food cake, or fruit for the chocolate fondue are fine. Prepare bite-size pieces as close to party time as possible. Squeezing fresh lemon juice over fruit prevents it from turning brown. When it comes time to make the dips, be careful 'cause this stuff gets hot!

Miss Swiss Cheese Fondue

serves 6-8

What You Need:

* 12 ounces mild Swiss cheese (mix in shredded cheddar if you like)
* 4 tablespoons all-purpose flour
* 1/4 teaspoon ground nutmeg
* 1 clove of garlic, cut in half
* 3 tablespoons butter
* 2-1/4 to 2-1/2 cups milk

* fresh lemon juice, salt and pepper to taste
* measuring cups and spoons
* grater
* 2 small bowls
* heavy saucepan
* fondue pot (and Sterno can)
* an adult to help

What You Do:

1. Using a grater, grate the cheese into a small bowl. Mix with 1 tablespoon of the flour. Set aside. In a separate bowl, stir together the remaining three tablespoons of flour with the nutmeg.

2. About 20 minutes before you're ready to serve, rub the cut garlic on the inside and bottom of a heavy saucepan. Put the butter in the saucepan over medium-low heat until it melts. Stir in the flour-nutmeg mixture until it forms a smooth paste.

3. Add the milk a little at a time, and stir constantly until the sauce is creamy and warm. Add cheese a handful at a time, and continue to stir.

4. Once the cheese has melted, add lemon juice, salt and pepper to taste.

5. Now very carefully (get an adult to help), pour the melted cheese directly from the hot saucepan into a fondue pot. Set the fondue pot on a stand over a lit Sterno can. If you don't have a fondue pot, keep your saucepan on the stove top, at medium-low heat, and eat directly from the saucepan.

Serve With Any of These:

* bite-size pieces of crusty French or Italian bread
* cut-up raw carrots
* purple grapes
* cooked but crunchy broccoli and cauliflower
* cut-up chunks of green apple

To Eat:

Spear a bite-size veggie, fruit, or chunk of bread, and carefully twirl it in the cheese, coating it completely. The cheese might be extremely hot, so make sure it's cool enough to eat before putting it in your mouth! Also, stock up on some regular or sparkling apple cider. Serving cider with fondue is a tradition.

Super Veggie Salad

serves 6-8

What You Need:

- ✳ 2 bags pre-packaged mixed salad greens
- ✳ 1 bunch fresh broccoli
- ✳ 1 bunch fresh cauliflower
- ✳ 1 large red, yellow, and orange peppers
- ✳ 1 pint cherry tomatoes
- ✳ fave salad dressing
- ✳ large serving bowl
- ✳ knife
- ✳ salad tongs

What You Do:

1. To make this colorful mixed salad—a great side dish for fondue—pour the mixed greens from the bag into a large serving bowl.

2. Wash the broccoli and cauliflower, and cut into florets. Slice the peppers into strips. Halve the tomatoes.

3. Toss all the ingredients together with the mixed greens. Serve with a favorite dressing.

Chocolate Dessert Fondue

serves 6-8

What You Need:

- ✳ 12 ounces semi sweet chocolate chips or Hershey bar pieces
- ✳ 1 cup light cream or half-and-half
- ✳ 1 teaspoon vanilla extract
- ✳ saucepan
- ✳ wooden spoon
- ✳ fondue pot (and Sterno can)
- ✳ an adult to help

What You Do:

1. Put the chocolate and light cream in a saucepan and cook slowly over low heat, stirring the whole time.

2. Once the chocolate is melted, add the vanilla extract and stir.

3. Transfer the melted chocolate from the saucepan to the fondue pot, with an adult's help, being careful not to spill any of the hot liquid. If you don't have a fondue pot, keep your saucepan on the stove top and carefully eat directly from the saucepan.

Serve With Any of These:

* sliced apples
* pineapple chunks
* halved strawberries
* banana slices

* pieces of angel food or pound cake
* marshmallows
* pieces of brownies

It's a Wrap!

This party's not over—it's only just begun! There's only one truly good excuse for throwing a great get-together—you want to have fun, fun, fun! That means you can host the bash of the century...just because. And throughout this book you've seen how to have a great time doing it! So go on—what are you waiting for? Pick a party, any party, and get planning. Grab some paper and a pen, and make out your guest list. No party poopers permitted!

Credits

When we first had the idea for *The Girls' Life Guide to Great Parties*, we hardly knew how we'd pack all the parties in. But we managed! What you are holding in your hands is, we think, the best of *GL's* best over nine years.

I would like to give major thanks to those whose talents made this book—and who make *GL*—great. As they say, behind every great magazine is a super talented team of editors, writers, and designers. And, for the past nine years, *GL* has been lucky enough to have some of the best. Thanks a million to executive editor Kelly White, Chun Kim, Sarah Cordi, Georgia Wilson, and Debbie Chaillou. Thanks, too, to Susan Bishansky, Lindsay Morgan, Andrea Reber and all of the great folks at Scholastic. We never could've done this without you!

Chapter 1: *Be a Girl with a Party Plan* (Kelly White and Michelle Silver); *Party Dilemma Sidebar* (Jodi Bryson)

Chapter 2: *No More Wallflower Hour* (Kelly White)

Chapter 3: *In the Mood for Food* (Kelly White); *Arctic Chocolate Pie Recipe* (Anne Vassal)

Chapter 4: *Super Slumber Parties* (Kelly White); *15 Fun Things to Do All Party Long With Your Friends* (Katy Myery, Lizzie Ross, Tish Daniels, and Beth Ann Sommerville); *Party Smarty* (Ellen Pill)

Chapter 5: *Best Birthday Bashes* (Michelle Silver and Kelly White); *Dreamy Ice Cream Recipes* (Anne Vassal); *Gifted and Grateful* (Sally VanDeventer)

Chapter 6: *Happy Holiday Celebrations A Sugar-'n'-Spice Soirée* (Muffy Fenwick); *Halloween Scream!* (Marcia S. Gresko and Kelly White); *Mega New Year's Eve Bash* (Cherish Wise, Kelly White, and Michelle Silver); *A Valentine Night Spa for the Girls* (Sarah Cordi and Cherish Wise); *Party Gras* (Jennifer Lawrence)

Chapter 7: *Terrific Theme Festivities Tea Party* (Kelly White and Kendi O'Neill); *Fall Fest* (Sarah Cordi); *Fun-Do Fest* (Sarah Cordi)